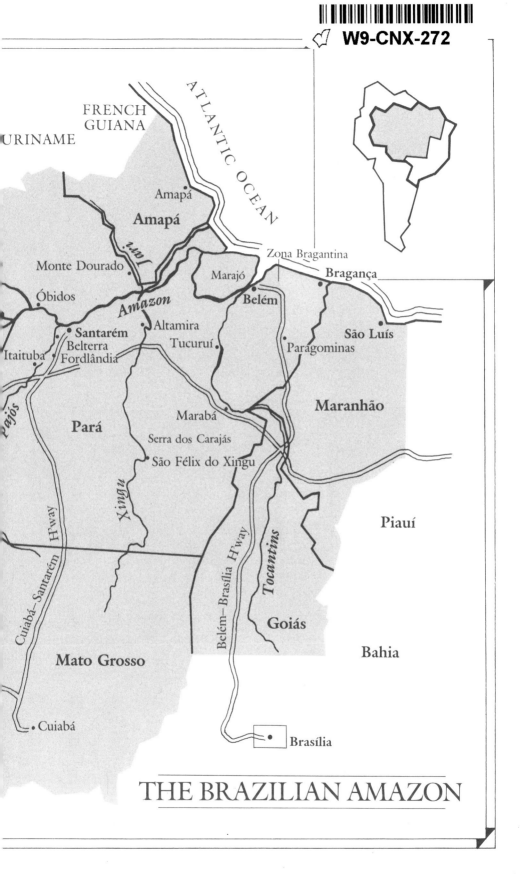

URINAME

FRENCH
GUIANA

ATLANTIC OCEAN

Amapá

Amapá

Jari

Zona Bragantina

Monte Dourado

Marajó

Bragança

Óbidos

Amazon

Belém

Santarém

Altamira

São Luís

Belterra
Fordlândia

Tucuruí

Paragominas

Itaituba

Tapajós

Marabá

Maranhão

Pará

Serra dos Carajás

São Félix do Xingu

Xingu

Piauí

Cuiabá–Santarém H'way

Belém–Brasília H'way

Tocantins

Goiás

Mato Grosso

Bahia

Cuiabá

Brasília

THE BRAZILIAN AMAZON

DREAMS OF
AMAZONIA

DREAMS OF AMAZONIA

Roger D. Stone

Elisabeth Sifton Books
VIKING

ELISABETH SIFTON BOOKS · VIKING
Viking Penguin Inc., 40 West 23rd Street,
New York, New York 10010, U.S.A.
Penguin Books Ltd, Harmondsworth,
Middlesex, England
Penguin Books Australia Ltd, Ringwood,
Victoria, Australia
Penguin Books Canada Limited, 2801 John Street,
Markham, Ontario, Canada L3R 1B4
Penguin Books (N.Z.) Ltd, 182–190 Wairau Road,
Auckland 10, New Zealand

First published in 1985 by Viking Penguin Inc.
Published simultaneously in Canada

LIBRARY OF CONGRESS CATALOGING IN PUBLICATION DATA
Stone, Roger.
    Dreams of Amazonia.
    "Elisabeth Sifton books."
    Bibliography: p.
    Includes index.
    1. Amazon River Valley—Description and travel.
    2. Stone, Roger. I. Title.
    F2546.S83 1985   981'.1   84-13091
    ISBN 0-670-11533-9

Grateful acknowledgment is made to the following for permission to reprint copyrighted material:

American Association for the Advancement of Science: "Speciation in Amazonian Forest Birds," by
J. Haffer, from *Science,* 165: 131–137, July 11, 1969. Copyright © 1969 by the American Association for the Advancement of Science.

Harvard University Press: From *Red Gold: The Conquest of the Brazilian Indians 1500–1760,* by
John Hemming. Published by Harvard University Press, 1978.

The Royal Historical Society, London, U.K.: Fifteen lines from *The Voyage of Pedro Teixeira on the
Amazon from Para to Quito and Back 1637–39,* by the Reverend George Edmundson, presented in
a paper to the Royal Historical Society in November 1920, series 4, volume 3.

Professor David Graham Sweet: Selections from "A Rich Realm of Nature Destroyed: The Middle
Amazon Valley, 1640–1750," the University of Wisconsin, Ph.D. dissertation, Modern History.
Copyright © 1975 Professor David Graham Sweet.

Map by Leon Auerbach Design Associates
Printed in the United States of America
by R. R. Donnelley & Sons Company, Harrisonburg, Virginia
Set in Galliard

FOREWORD

Saul Steinberg once made a wonderful series of drawings about the various ways to get from A to B. One has a straight line. Another has a line with slight undulations. A third line breaks, abruptly, into a rhythmic series of angry, jagged diagonals. In a fourth, which at home we used to call the John Profumo model in honor of the prominent British gentleman who during the 1960s had a sudden and notorious affair with a woman "beneath his station," the line proceeds straight from A almost all the way to B. Then it erupts into a frenzied maze before resuming its steady course.

The trajectory of this book is a long one. I began to think about the Amazon and its development back in the 1960s, during my tour of duty as chief of the Time-Life News Bureau in Rio de Janeiro. The conventional wisdom of the time, which I believed, was that the region probably contained vast oil reserves and had, as well, the potential to become a breadbasket for the world. Though I was wrong to believe that, I did learn some useful things about political, economic, and social trends in Brazil. I also approached mastery of Portuguese, a Chinese puzzle of a language full of booby traps like the future subjunctive tense, and developed great admiration and fondness for the people of Brazil and their unique culture.

Later I saw Brazil through different filters—as an international banking functionary, as head of a small nonprofit organization concerned with inter-American relations, and most recently as a board (later staff) member of World Wildlife Fund–U.S. It was here, beginning in 1976, that I found my way into tropical ecology and toward some understanding of the intricate vulnerability and global significance of the Amazonian forest. In 1978 I began to think that a book could be made of the subject. In 1982, at last, I found an opportunity to begin a run at it.

My own passage from Starting Point A to Completion Point B can be compared with none of the Steinberg Variations, for he had no example to symbolize the many helping hands that have abetted my passage across the middle ground. There was, to begin with, the board of directors of what is now the Americas Society/Center for Inter-American Relations, which kindly provided me with a leave of absence for preliminary travel, interviews, and library research. Next, chronologically, came Elisabeth Sifton of Viking Penguin, to whom I owe very special gratitude for her recognition, amid a cluttered field of book ideas and proposals, of my subject's merit, as well as for her uncanny ability to spot jargon or banality. During the past year, as I have shirked other duties in order to complete my research and writing, my colleagues at World Wildlife Fund–U.S.—in particular, our president, Russell E. Train—have shown remarkable tolerance. Anna C. Roosevelt, of the Museum of the American Indian in New York, kindly lent me many useful books.

Financial support from the Armand G. Erpf Fund enabled me to undertake the recent travel to Amazonia that resulted in much of the firsthand material presented here. Most importantly, the Fund's much-appreciated backing brought about the participation of Katherine Caraccioli as research assistant during the critical phases of refining and checking the manuscript. Katherine's cheerful and careful comments and reactions, rendered on the basis of her extensive experience in scientific and technical research, have been essential to the project. I'm thankful also to Thomas E. Lovejoy, Mary C. Pearl, Riordan Roett, and Susanna B. Hecht for their most useful comments on various parts of the manuscript. During the drafting process Ellen Arntz was the good-natured recipient of countless floppy diskettes (before 1983, I hardly knew what one was) from which she performed almost daily the small miracle of extracting printed chunks of material. Vasda B. Landers helped assure the accuracy and proper punctuation of the occasional sprinkles of Portuguese in the text.

There are no people I admire more than all of those who, from every standpoint, continue to study the dilemmas and paradoxes of Amazonia and, against lengthening odds, search for sustainable solutions. If the forests of the basin are in fact redeemed from the eventual disappearance that I foresee, their pioneering work will have been chiefly responsible. It is their devotion and their accomplishments, rather than personal derring-do of the sort that has characterized most Amazonian literature since Friar Gaspar de Carvajal published his breathless account of the first European descent of the river in 1542, that I have tried to highlight most brightly here. Many of these people have been most generous with their time in interviews and conversations, have sent papers and articles, have suggested sources of further information, and in countless other ways have been essential to the project. I hesitate to mention particular individuals for fear of overlooking others, and simply offer my deep thanks to all those who with great patience have helped me to try to understand the workings of the Amazonian ecosystem.

On my journey from A to B, I have, in short, been helped by many people (none, I should add before closing, more than Flo and Leslie, my wife and daughter), and have seen Amazonia through many pairs of eyes. I thank them all, and wish you well as you embark upon this curious passage.

ROGER D. STONE
Cornwall-on-Hudson, N.Y.
June 1984

CONTENTS

DREAMS OF
AMAZONIA

CHAPTER 1
Looking for the Doido

TWENTY YEARS AGO I FIRST VISITED AMAZONIA. ON ITS LANDING AP-
proach to Manaus, 1,600 kilometers westward from the mouth of the river,
the twin-jet Caravelle passed over the Encontro das Águas (Meeting of the
Waters), that point where the black Rio Negro and the pale, muddy Solimões
converge to form a single massive stream. For maybe a kilometer the two
colors of fast-flowing water boil along separately beside each other, forming
curling and twining patterns at the border, where fish frolic and terns flutter
and swoop, before finally merging into uniform *café au lait*. The incongruous
opera house in Manaus, built at the height of the *belle époque* rubber boom in
the region, was then painted rosy pink and not its current battleship gray.
Slums consisting of nests of floating boats ("*cidades flutuantes*") cluttered the
edge of the town. Ashore, little was stirring. I saw a white-elephant steel mill
and at midday strolled on uncrowded streets where women walked with um-
brellas unfurled against the hot sun. I went to Belém at the river's mouth, and
one morning called on the United States Consul-General. He invited me to
join him for cocktails later that day and proposed that we meet at the town's
most elegant whorehouse so that I would have a chance to meet a good

selection of prominent citizens and politicians. I went to São Luís do Maranhão, an island city at the very eastern end of Amazonia, and there found
little changed from the seventeenth century. Some fine churches and old colonial buildings, little frequented, were there to see. Not much was going on;
the labor-intensive cotton industry had died soon after Brazil's Emancipation,
in 1888. My 5:00 A.M. flight, then the only way out by air each day, had
already departed when I arrived at the airport at 4:35. Like a good *gringo* I
threw a fit, but it did no good.

This illustration from Alfred Russel Wallace's *Travels on the Amazon and Rio
Negro* seems remarkably like the upper Rio Negro and the Uaupés today.

These sleepy and unpromising places I first knew during the 1960s. Early
in my discovery of Amazonia, I also got onto the water—up the Solimões
(the midsection of the Amazon above Manaus) with Senator Robert Kennedy,
to the beautiful Anavilhanas Archipelago up the Rio Negro from Manaus, an
excursion aboard one of those double-decker river vessels where travelers sling
hammocks and watch and doze as they saunter along past the endless shore.
Once I took a photograph that showed a small canoe in the foreground. The
rest of the picture, of which the boat forms only a small image in one lower
corner, consists of flat-calm river. I drove out to the northwestern frontier of
Rondônia, later to become a beehive of colonization activity, but then an
empty wilderness accessible only by one dirt road that had just been opened.
Indians had attacked the construction workers with bows and arrows; we saw

a man with an empty eye socket, who had been a victim of such an incident.

In the 1970s I went often to Brazil, and heard much about how new programs for crash development, in Amazonia as well as in the south, would produce quick results for this now impatient "land of tomorrow." During those years I also came to know a number of scientists at work in Amazonia. I visited them at their field stations in the forest, as well as in their laboratories, and began to appreciate their studies of an intricate world still mostly unknown. They told me of their fascination with their work, instructed me in elementary Amazonian ecology, tried to make me understand how priceless and how threatened was this vast and empty, green and watery part of the planet. Altogether, by the 1980s I had been exposed to many sides of Amazonia. But I had still not ever visited a corner of it where things were more or less as they had been before Europeans arrived during the sixteenth century, where the modern world had made no headway. Clearly it was important for anyone seeking to understand what there was to preserve in Amazonia, and what development placed in jeopardy, to undergo such an experience.

The place I selected was a black river called the Uaupés, in the northwest corner of Brazil. It flows past dense tropical forest into the upper Rio Negro, the northernmost of the two principal rivers that form the Amazon far downstream. The mouth of the Uaupés is about eight miles north of 0°0′ latitude. The nearest town is called São Gabriel da Cachoeira (St. Gabriel of the Rapids). Margaret Mee, a diminutive and strong-willed septuagenarian botanical artist who has long traveled the Amazon basin to collect and paint orchids and other plants, had heard from a Brazilian highway department pilot, and passed the news along to me, that certain villages along the Uaupés are "little changed if at all." The Indians of the region, protected by Salesian missionaries and a federal bureau of Indian affairs called FUNAI, are carefully shielded. Technically, at least, their villages are off limits to those who have no business there.

The nineteenth-century explorer and naturalist Alfred Russel Wallace, an Englishman who worked with Darwin in the formulation of his theory of natural selection, was "attacked by fever" on the Uaupés in 1852 and forced to take to his hammock in a hamlet called São Joaquim, near the mouth of the river. "I could eat nothing," he wrote. He was "so torpid and helpless that Senhor L., who attended me, did not expect me to live." Another British visitor of that same year was the sickly, white-bearded botanist Richard Spruce. So fearful of malaria that he huddled inside the *tolda* (cabin) of his boat at night without venturing on deck and scornful even of São Gabriel ("a wretched place—never is there so much as an egg or a banana to be had for love or money"), Spruce nevertheless ventured far up the Uaupés. Wallace, too, recovered from his illness and fought his way through a succession of rapids, north and west along the Uaupés toward Colombia. He visited places never before seen by any European. Both he and Spruce wrote voluminously of their adventures on the Uaupés and of the "rich and novel" species of the region.

So another reason for choosing the Uaupés was to follow in the footsteps of these illustrious pioneers, whose journals (along with that of the entomologist Henry Walter Bates) constitute classics of their kind. I also wanted to

An early rendering of the Amazonian *igapó*, or flooded forest. Note the typically Amazonian root structure of the trees.

see the Uaupés because of the paradox of its biology. I had read of the magnificence of the tropical foliage that borders the Uaupés and, as well, of the infertility that the trees disguise. The river's waters, like those of New Jersey's Pine Barrens, run through white-sand regions dating from ancient geological times, and from which almost all nutrients were leached millions of years ago. Distilled water is only slightly purer than what can be scooped from the Uaupés. Since both the soils and the waters of the region contain so little life-supporting material, the biota (plants and animals) there is scarce and strangely diverse. Although there are many species, the total number of birds and animals is far lower than in other parts of Amazonia; even insects are in relatively short supply. The trees themselves survive and grow to great heights only because they are all but totally closed systems: through a variety of intricate mechanisms, they recapture and recycle almost all of the nutrients stored within them. Mostly they feed on themselves.

Betty J. Meggers, an eminent anthropologist and archaeologist who has studied Amazonia since the 1940s, said of places like the Uaupés in her classic 1971 book, *Amazonia: Man and Nature in a Counterfeit Paradise*: "The oxygen-deprived, acid, sterile aquatic environment of this flooded forest, or *igapó*, is one of the most remarkable and little-studied ecological niches of Amazonia. From the standpoint of human exploitation, the black water rivers and the land they drain have such low subsistence potential that they are notorious throughout Amazonia as 'starvation rivers.'"

It was this strange and distant place, then, that I selected as a way to find a different Amazonia. I went there in late 1983. Here is the diary of my brief trip, which began at Manaus:

Tuesday, October 11

I am up at 3:30 A.M. to check out of my hotel, half an hour outside of Manaus on the Rio Negro. The driver of my cab (a VW bug, here called a *fusca*) has been persuaded to wait for me all night in the hotel parking lot. He emerges drowsily from the back seat, where he has been sleeping, and we set off through empty streets (once swerving sharply to avoid a dog sleeping in the middle of the highway) to INPA, Brazil's National Amazon Research Institute. There we pick up Judith Gunn. She is a University of Wisconsin graduate student in cultural geography, and she wants to come with me if she can wheedle her way aboard the fully booked plane to São Gabriel, on which I have a confirmed reservation. The eighteen-seat Bandeirante, a Brazilian-made, twin-engined turboprop, flies from Manaus to São Gabriel only three times a week. The flight is said always to be loaded to its weight limit with a combination of people, mail, and freight. At 5:00 A.M. we are at the airline counter inside the airport, in ample time, we think, for Judith to get her name on the very top of the *"lista de espera."* But she is distressed to discover that someone has beaten us to the punch. Later we find him, an amiable blond man, approaching middle age, who is reading a comic book.

Judith and I have both made elaborate preparations for a journey during which, we assume, others will be able to extend little help. We have with us hammocks, sheets for the surprisingly chilly Amazonian evenings, mosquito nets and repellent, dried foods, a small pot, plates and forks and knives and spoons, raingear, soap, and towels. We envision that we will be able to charter a small canoe and a boatman, and that we will camp on the white-sand beaches that appear around the upper Rio Negro when the water is low. For Judith, though, the effort is for the moment wasted. All expected passengers show up, and even the comic-book man is turned away. Before we part (Judith is more cheerful than I would be under the circumstances), we agree that she will try to make the next flight, two days hence, and join me in São Gabriel. I borrow a spoon from her and set off. It is hot and humid aboard the plane. We stop once at Barcelos, on the Rio Negro, a town surrounded by the curious, permanently flooded *igapó*. By around ten-thirty, after two hours and forty minutes of flying time, during which I've been rereading portions of Wallace's delightful *Travels on the Amazon and Rio Negro*, we are gliding down over thick forest toward the inland airstrip that serves São Gabriel. As we descend we pass high, rocky hills reminiscent of Rio de Janeiro's famous Sugarloaf, though not quite so dramatic.

Aeroporto do Uaupés, says the sign painted on the wall of the little terminal shack. Outside there are two taxis, both *fuscas*. As my driver I choose Vanduir, or more precisely, this pleasant-faced young man chooses me. He is, I learn, an emigrant from the impoverished state of Ceará, in the dry northeast quadrant of Brazil. There is a second passenger in the car when Vanduir tosses in my baggage, a young man carrying a Samsonite brief case. I ask him how things are in São Gabriel. "Bad," he says, with no amplification. Vanduir is cheerier. In addition to being the owner-driver of his taxi, he works at the post office part time and has other odd jobs as well. He rents a little apartment in the building that houses the town's only restaurant, he tells me, and his central location gets him involved in many projects. Vanduir is making a far better living, he says, than he would if he had stayed in his home town of Fortaleza. His only real complaint: *"Pega mulher, todo mundo sabe"*—you date a girl, and the whole town knows about it.

We continue along the smooth red dirt road toward town. En route, we reach an intersection with an arrow and a sign wryly indicating a nonexistent road to Manaus. Vanduir says that there are nine thousand people in the whole *município* of São Gabriel, and four thousand within the town. That is many more people than Judith and I had anticipated. São Gabriel has a hospital with

two doctors, Vanduir continues, and a *colégio*, or high school, run by the
Salesian mission and so well attended that no student can go for more than
half a day. It is now midday, and droves of them in clean uniforms, most
appearing to be at least partially Indian, are walking on the roads. Passing
through the unpaved streets of the town, I note that sprawl has already begun
even here. The dirt roads seem to reach randomly toward the forest, and small
wood or mud houses are scattered helter-skelter along them.

We reach the Rio Negro and the *cachoeira* where the tea-brown water in
the shallows boils into dirty white surf as it surges over rocks and shoals near
the shore. Here the river is not wide, and on the other side the green forest
tumbles down to the water's edge. In the distance are more high mountains,
standing in sharp contrast to the gently rolling hills that are more typical of
the Amazonian lowland forest. Vanduir takes me to the only hotel, a two-
story affair with several beds in each room. A number of rough-looking char-
acters (gold prospectors?) have checked in just ahead of me, and I am not
greatly sorry to hear that every bed is taken. I abandon the idea of spending
the first night in São Gabriel and ask Vanduir if he could help me find a boat
to take me to the Uaupés right away. Driving along the shore, we see the
sorts of boat that might be available ranged before us in a back eddy out of

'Zé Maria's *tolda* (Roger D. Stone)

the current, their bows pulled up on a muddy bank—various small dugout canoes, some with outboard motors and some with low, thatched *toldas* over the after sections of their hulls, and several somewhat more substantial vessels, with larger *toldas* and diesel motors. Vanduir says that there is a good chance I can charter one of these bigger boats for a few days, and cruises slowly along the waterfront in search of one of the skippers. Almost instantly he finds one. "I'm busy and tomorrow is a holiday," the man says. "But try 'Zé Maria—he isn't doing anything."

We set off again, past a small commercial section where there are stores with names like Bazar Cearense, and down a steep grade of road that descends right into the Rio Negro. At the end an unnamed, unpainted, sturdy-looking boat, beamy and about ten meters long, comes into view. It is fully enclosed by a cabin and has a thatched roof over which a couple of pieces of corrugated metal have been casually slung. Out in the open, in the after section of the cabin, is a bright green, new-looking engine. No one seems to be around. Then there is a splash, a slight young man with a scraggly beard and twinkling eyes maneuvers around the bow of the boat, towing a log. 'Zé (short for José) Maria has been found. I explain that I do not have a destination, but would like to explore as far up the Uaupés as possible, arrange a rendezvous with Judith, and maybe see some of the Rio Negro too. Although 'Zé Maria seems

The crew. Left to right: Luís, 'Zé Maria, Faustino *(Roger D. Stone)*

not quite able to comprehend that I don't have to *get* anywhere, we agree on a per diem price before he has even emerged from the water, and plan our departure for early afternoon.

There are minor delays while I reconfirm my flight back to Manaus and eat lunch in the restaurant where Vanduir lives. It has a dance floor decorated with hanging Indian feather ornaments and a wheezing sound system whose principal offering, appropriately, is Paul Simon's "Bridge over Troubled Waters." 'Zé Maria goes off to round up his crew, which turns out to consist of his younger brother Luís as boatswain and cook, and a stocky, salt-and-pepper-haired, nut-brown *caboclo*, an Amazonian of mixed Indian and white blood, named Faustino da Silva, as helmsman and navigator. With little enthusiasm 'Zé Maria accepts my offering of dried Knorr soup (part of our deal is that meals are on his account) and sends for his own supply of food. Luís rolls aboard a full tank of propane gas and hooks it up to the battered stove that rests on a platform aft of the engine. We arrange with Vanduir to meet Judith on the Thursday flight and dispatch her on a fast outboard to meet me on the Uaupés, thus sparing the rest of us from having to claw our way upstream, then lose all distance gained against the current by returning to São Gabriel to fetch Judith there. Even without planning a return to São Gabriel, we would have to travel for thirty-six hours to reach the first of many *cachoeiras* farther upstream that are mentioned in Spruce's journal, *Notes of a Botanist*.

By midafternoon we are on the point of casting off when a battered blue Volkswagen hatchback lurches to a halt on the road above. Out steps a trimly uniformed young cop who boards our boat, demands a look at my passport and landing card, and asks me what other documents I have that authorize my visit to the São Gabriel region. This is a national security area, and the police and the military run things. I must undergo a *fiscalização* (inspection). Although I have no other official documents with me, I had been forewarned by Margaret Mee of the possibility of this sort of harassment, and upon her advice had written a letter (in my less than fully grammatical Portuguese) to her acquaintance Colonel Dárcio Ribeiro Machado in Rio de Janeiro. The idea was that Colonel Dárcio would arrange a laissez-passer for me from the senior general in Manaus, but this had not happened. The cop is not impressed by the photocopy of my letter to Colonel Dárcio, and says that I will have to go with him both to the *delegacia*, or police station, and to the military command post. Probably, he adds, they will have to radio Manaus, if not Brasília as well, for my clearance.

Somber thoughts flash. Am I to be accused of being a smuggler or CIA agent or agitator among the Indians? Or worse? At the very least, will the delay involved be long enough to end my dream of seeing the Uaupés? I am on a tight schedule and must be back in São Gabriel by Saturday. The cop loads me into the Volkswagen. Fenders flapping, it rattles uphill and stops neither at the *delegacia* nor at the military headquarters, but at the hospital. I am left in the outpatient waiting room, with several mothers and sniffling young children, to ponder the possibility of an immediate torture session. After ten anxious minutes I am led into a dentist's office and introduced to a man whose T-shirt says he is Captain Sarmento. He greets me smilingly. Surely this is a bluff, I think—out will come my teeth, one by one, until I confess. The captain asks me a few simple questions. Then he extends his arms to shake hands and says, *"Boa viagem"*—have a good trip. The cop seems crestfallen at my victory and wordlessly drives me back to the river. I wonder why the dentist represents ultimate authority in São Gabriel.

It is midafternoon and hot. 'Zé Maria hits the starter and the green diesel, which turns out to be of Chinese manufacture ("Cheaper," 'Zé Maria grunts), gurgles smartly into action. Luís, age twenty-one, slight like 'Zé Maria and with a pleasant and impish expression, casts off. At the helm far forward, Faustino bangs a long bolt against a metal winch handle beside him, and thus sends gear and throttle signals back to 'Zé Maria, stationed by the motor. One ding and we are in forward gear. With two dings on Faustino's "engine-order telegraph" we accelerate and at last are moving up the Rio Negro toward the Uaupés. The scenery is splendid. Hard-running water, black where it is deep and the color of pale Coca-Cola in the shallows, pushes against the many rocks and sandbars in the river. Here it is perhaps a kilometer wide. Two handsome species of swallow, the white-winged and the black-banded, flutter and twitter about the rocks. High, bold mountain ranges lie ahead and astern. The thick forest tumbles down to the water's edge. Here there seems to be far less variation from high to low water than exists elsewhere in the basin, where flooding may have become more pronounced because of instability resulting from deforestation. Suddenly an osprey flies from its still perch on a dead treetop, swoops down, and snags a small fish in its talons.

As we slog along upstream, making no more than two or three knots against the swift current, I make a rough inventory of what there is aboard: Faustino's battery-powered shortwave radio, candles, bananas, salt, dried soups, a Colombian flag, several pots and pans, soap, two flashlights of which one is the powerful kind that uses six batteries, two empty fuel drums and a full one far aft, soybean oil, hammocks, some empty tin cans. I ask 'Zé Maria what, besides the foodstuffs in sight, he might have in mind for us to eat. "I hope you like fish," he says.

Like many people from the northeast of Brazil, 'Zé Maria is *fechado*—close-mouthed. Even so, I manage to extract from him the essentials of his life to date. He is the eldest of nine children—six sons, three daughters. When he reached young adulthood he felt the need to escape from the northeast, where he saw no future. He went first to Belém, which now has a population of more than one million and is the basin's largest urban center. From there, 'Zé

Maria moved inland to spend five years in the gold-trading boomtown of Itaituba, on the Tapajós, a sparkling clear-water river that flows from the south into the Amazon at Santarém, eight hundred kilometers west of Belém. 'Zé Maria fared well at Itaituba, but he tired of it: "I felt I was a prisoner of the highway there. I wanted to spend my time closer to the water." He continued westward, found São Gabriel, and liked it. In only two and one-half years he has acquired a house in São Gabriel and installed there his wife and several children. Luís travels with 'Zé Maria and seems to live aboard the boat, even though he talks vaguely of having a place ashore. A third brother, younger than Luís, has arrived recently and works in the *comercio*. The family's last name, I finally discover, is Diosios.

'Zé Maria's boat, built in Manaus of sturdy Amazonian hardwoods, is still so new that the planking is not fully swelled. Pumping is a frequent necessity. But this turns out to be the only major difficulty with 'Zé Maria's boat— fortunately, for this is his livelihood. He is an old-style river trader. Each year he and his crew make numerous voyages of two weeks or so, usually up the Rio Negro to the town of San Carlos in Venezuela (which was the closest to the Amazon, thanks to hostile authorities in Brazil, that the famous German explorer Baron Alexander von Humboldt ever reached). He will buy and sell "anything"—clothes, bulk food, tricycles, Bell's Scotch whiskey, outboard motors. He maintains a substantial inventory in a warehouse in São Gabriel and occasionally travels to Manaus (four days down, five back) to stock up. The prices he pays for these goods are already far over the national norms, since almost everything he buys is imported from southern Brazil, and they reach celestial levels when he adds his own markup. But he seems to have little difficulty finding customers. In his pocket he carries a fat wad of 5,000-cruzeiro notes (each, at this writing, worth U.S. $5.10 on what is euphemistically referred to as the "parallel" market), and he is sufficiently liquid to be able to accept some payments not in cash but in barter goods or gold dust. The latter is increasingly being found in the rivers above São Gabriel, particularly in one called the Içana, and it trades for between ten and twelve thousand cruzeiros a gram. "I know everybody on these rivers," 'Zé Maria says matter-of-factly. I begin to think that I have made a good find.

Evening is coming. We see occasional Indian fishermen drifting in their canoes, hand-lining. Settlements are widely scattered. On the river there are no aids to navigation, and the rocks and sandbars present hazards even in full daylight. For the first of many times I marvel at Faustino's ability to avoid the obstacles that lie hidden beneath the surface. We draw about a meter, and at that depth the water's color is already approaching ink-black. It is fully night, the only light that of a crisp half moon, when we finally tie up to the root of a tree alongside an island near where the Uaupés and the Negro meet. Dinner consists of rice, hard *farinha* (a tooth-jarring Amazonian staple that is made from the manioc root), and a hashlike, reddish canned meat substance that Luís has barely warmed. A whole onion (slice-your-own) provides seasoning. We eat sitting on the floorboards amidships. Soon afterward we are in our hammocks, listening to country music (voices and an accordion) coming from Faustino's radio. Then Radio São Gabriel da Cachoeira announces its "Messenger of the Air" service, which, in the absence of any other form of communication, links townspeople with their friends and relatives in the hinterlands. Sample messages:

"Maria da Conceição da Silva died today at the hospital in São Gabriel. Aunt Sílvia is in a state of shock."

"I could not buy all the things for the *festa* because I did not have enough money. I am coming home tomorrow."

"Uncle João says he cannot lend you the money. All well here. *Abraços.*"

I doze as the radio plays on. My mind turns to a subject hardly likely to induce heavy sleep: vampire bats. Spruce had found São Gabriel "terribly infested" with them, and his own house not immune. "When I entered it," he wrote, "there were large patches of dried-up blood on the floor which had been drawn from my predecessors....My two men were attacked the first night, one of them having wounds on the ends of his toes.... The bats do not stop at the toes, but bite occasionally on the legs, fingers' ends, nose and chin and forehead, especially of children." Janet Chernella, a graduate student in anthropology at Columbia, recently did fieldwork from a base in São Gabriel. Although she took elaborate antibat precautions, she reports having occasionally awoken with "bloody socks." 'Zé Maria has hardly consoled me by saying that the bats not only occur in São Gabriel but are common in the entire region. I refuse not to sleep barefoot, but I carefully wrap my toes within my sheet. Even so, I feel them once and convince myself that they are wet. This turns out to be a false alarm. During the night, though, I am distinctly aware of a whir of wings entering the cabin from the open forward end, and exiting from the open bay amidships.

Wednesday, October 12

Before dawn I hear people walking down the riverbank, and the sounds of a canoe being paddled out into the stream. I wonder what sort of urgent errand could prompt them (whoever they are) to start the day so early. Later, at five o'clock, Faustino's radio begins a country music serenade. Breakfast (sweet black coffee, small oval crackers, canned butter) arrives at dawn. While we are eating, the canoe returns. Aboard are Indians: an old man, two younger women, one little girl of about five. Faustino seems to know them well, and there is rapid conversation as they tie up alongside us. "We've been looking for the *doido* (madman)," says the old man. "He left our village and no one has seen him for three days." One of the women, who wears a blue cotton frock, has a pained expression. "He's always been crazy," she says. "Once he tore off all my clothes and left me naked in the forest." "He's very dangerous," says the other woman. "He has threatened to kill people before, and maybe he wants to kill people now. Maybe he wants to kill all of us. He must be found." A machete and a gun are lying in the bottom of the canoe. It is not clear whether the *doido* is an Indian, a *caboclo*, or an outsider.

Soon after sunrise we are under way. After an hour we stop at a place called Santa Teresinha, a settlement that, as we shall discover, is typical of the region. It has perhaps a dozen families in residence, each in a single-story house with a thatched roof, hardened mud walls, and a dirt floor. A central square, large enough for children to play *futebol* (soccer), is the focal point; at its sides are a school and a church run by a Portuguese *padre*, one of the few people around who is neither Indian nor *caboclo*. Pigs wander freely about the compound, and there are many kinds of fruit trees. 'Zé Maria buys a two-and-a-half-pound catfish from a *caboclo* resident of the village. He also buys a dozen green coconuts. Not many people are visible. This is a holiday and there is a special *dia da criança*, or children's festival, in São Gabriel. Many families have paddled off to attend the festivities—half a day down, a full day back up. No one reckons distance by kilometers here; it is only a question of hours or days. 'Zé Maria seems less than fully interested in the maps I have with me. We ask about the *doido*. No one has seen him, but we discover at least that he belongs to the same Indian group as those searching for him.

Off again, under cloudy skies, at midmorning. Luís takes the catfish, known locally as a *piraíba*, and quarters it on the fantail. He removes much fatty tissue from inside the fish, a species that Wallace called "fat and delicious" but that made him "very ill with dysentery and continued pains in the stomach" after he had eaten it "three or four times consecutively without vegetable food." 'Zé Maria is sitting cross-legged on the open bow, scraping the rough edges of his toes with a razor blade. Faustino mans the wheel, often making sudden movements as the current buffets us. A falcon (I cannot tell which species) makes three breathtaking swoops but fails to capture the small bird it is chasing. Remarkably, I learn later, these splendid little raptors score kills only about once in every ten tries. The coast is rocky as we swing from the Rio Negro into the Uaupés, whose mouth is studded with islands. If these evergreens had needles and not broad leaves, I think, we could be along the coast of Maine. But Maine has no such thing as a Greater Yellow-Headed Vulture. One soars by, its white underbelly clearly distinguishing it from a regular buzzard.

At ten o'clock we pass the tidy thatched village of São Joaquim, which took Spruce five days to reach from São Gabriel and where Wallace had his bout of fever. It seems little changed from its appearance at the time of their visits. Just beyond São Joaquim we stop at the isolated house of a trader known as "Cesário da Lancha"—Caesar of the Motorboat. He is a northeasterner with an Indian wife and a *caboclo* family. Adjacent to his small, trim house, painted white over the adobe, is a small warehouse full of goods, and a freshly painted boat is tied up a few steps from the front door. The dirt around the house has been newly swept, as has the dirt floor of its central "parlor" room. There we sit on several basic wooden chairs. A shortwave radio is the principal adornment. Conversation between Cesário and 'Zé Maria is punctuated by long silences. Much of the talk concerns the habits of the local Indian men, and Cesário offers a graphic tale of one recent knife duel. "They fight even without *cachaça* (the local rum)," says Cesário, an older black-haired man with rubber boots and many missing teeth. He adds that FUNAI, the much-disparaged Indian protection agency, "does not allow us to sell it to them, but somehow they get it anyway. You give them some and they are sure to fight. They don't know how to handle liquor. After three or four shots they are drunk." I sense no condescension about the way Cesário says these things, none of the scorn about drunken Indians that is part of the U.S. tradition. This is simply how Indians are, in his view. Cesário has not seen the *doido*.

We pass the middle of the day under way again, keeping close to the shore to reduce the effect of the current. It is all but windless and the water is calm, even though the river has now widened and there would be choppy waves in a heavy wind. Five small yellow butterflies, each following the other, pass by. We eat the excellent *piraíba*, fried in soybean oil, with none of the ill effects that befell poor Wallace. Soon after lunch we arrive at a hamlet called Trovão, which, according to a plaque prominently placed near the church, was founded by the Salesians in 1927. About twenty assorted Indian adults and children are gathered in front of the church. A stout wooden cross, perhaps seven meters in length, is lying on the ground and a man is digging a hole in which to insert it. Soon it will be raised in honor of Our Lady of Aparecida, the patron saint of Brazil, whose holy day this is. After the hole is made deep enough, everybody enters the little church. There is no padre present, though an itinerant one comes, from time to time, to perform sacraments. Now a crackly tape cassette, played on an ancient, battery-powered machine, leads the service.

There is a sweetness to the slightly off-key singing. Soon the men emerge again into the bright afternoon sunlight, and the women and children follow. With the help of two tall ladders that serve as guides, they raise the cross. Then four men place a replica of the saint, mounted between two long poles and standing before a cross, onto their shoulders. A firecracker explodes. A procession then moves from the church to the rocks by the water. After a blessing, the saint is placed aboard a motorized canoe. Two brightly beribboned

On the Uaupés. Indian elders prepare to launch a canoe carrying a likeness of Our Lady of Aparecida. *(Roger D. Stone)*

elders pilot her off upriver. The other villagers stand on the rocks and watch wave as the canoe and the saint grow smaller. I wonder where they plan to go.

We move back toward our boat, and most of the remaining Indians follow. They sit down in the shade of trees at the water's edge, and we talk. The fishing has not been good, and the meals lately have consisted mostly of rice and *farinha*. Little evidence is to be found here of the small kitchen-garden plots, called *roças*, that border most of these hamlets, and there is a general air of malaise. Trovão, we learn, has shrunk. Many people have died or have moved to São Gabriel or Manaus. We set off upriver. During the afternoon we stop at a small deserted farm to gather hot peppers. Later we take shelter in an *igarapé*, or little stream, while a heavy squall passes. I collect some rainwater and drink it. I am already accustomed to dipping a mug in the river; drinking colorless water seems peculiar. The trees are not high here, no more than one hundred feet at the maximum, but if we were towing a little canoe I would want to take it and paddle off into the *igapó* to search for the forest treasures that Spruce and Wallace found along here.

We arrive for the night at another mission called Cunuri. Nobody comes down to the boat. After supper, I translate Spruce to the crew. They laugh at the part about his sleeping inside the *tolda* to guard against malaria, which no longer exists around here, and are amused that Spruce could find neither an egg nor a banana in São Gabriel. Faustino, fifty-six and apparently a Romeo who has had affairs with many Indian women along the rivers, says that Spruce's elaborate description of Indian festivals still largely holds true. "They dance till they run out of *cachaça*," he says.

We talk of places and why I am here and where I have been and where I am going. I say that soon I am returning to the United States and describe how. 'Zé Maria is thunderstruck that I can get there aboard a Brazilian airliner. We deploy our hammocks. The resident rat, who lives in the *tolda*'s thatching, scuffles about. Luís, smoking roll-your-own cigarettes that he carefully fills with vile tobacco, repeatedly hawks and spits onto the cabin floor. Outside it rains steadily, but the *tolda* does not leak.

Thursday, October 13

Even before daylight has really come, such insects as there are have swung into action. I am bitten several times by an aggressive horsefly called the *motuca* that raises a large and temporarily painful welt. Church bells ring soon after dawn, and everybody in the village attends the Mass. A large cross lies on the ground in readiness for the Aparecida ceremony that here will take place this afternoon. Luís and 'Zé Maria collect green lemons from an abundantly fruiting tree. Parakeets squawk overhead. Occasional small flights of Amazonian parrots appear as well, but not the great flocks to be seen and heard each morning in many other parts of Amazonia. Nor does the macaw, of any creature the most symbolic of Amazonia, seem to occur here. Church ends and a few people drift over to the boat. All have heard that the *doido* is missing, but nobody has any news of him.

On upstream. Faustino explains that each of the Indian villages we are visiting contains people from five or six different tribes. The Toucanos have made it a law that any marriage must be with someone from outside their own fast-shrinking group. 'Zé Maria says, with a touch of regional pride, that it is not just a question of the dangers of interbreeding: "All the Indian girls want to go with a white man such as a northeasterner." Faustino chooses not to respond to this challenge.

The Indian places we have seen, such as Trovão and Cunuri, seem no more than fading settlements that would disappear quickly if FUNAI and the missionaries stopped caring for those lingering there. Now, though, we come to a different sort of an Indian village. São Pedro was founded only twelve years ago, after the death of an old man at his beautiful home on a nearby island in midstream. Following tradition, his family abandoned the site and moved slightly upstream. Little different in appearance or population from the other villages, São Pedro by chance became the beneficiary of a major prize on the Uaupés: a new school with a good teacher. Quickly it drew children from the surrounding region, who were sent here to board. Now São Pedro has a notably young population, and there is a pulsing rhythm to the children's laughter and games.

The men are busy here too, carving Brazil-wood crosses for their Aparecida day. Faustino stops at one house where the men are working, and drinks a bowl of *xibé*, a *farinha* soup. Here, one man says, fish abound in the river "except when the water is very high. Then we go to the forest to hunt for deer, peccaries, curassow birds, or monkeys." Round squashes, which I have seen nowhere else, are growing in one kitchen garden. But even here the sense of sadness and dependency is almost palpable. I ask a man if he goes often to São Gabriel. "No," he says. "We belong to the other big mission, up the river at Taraqua. That is where we go if we leave here. That is where our children go from the *primário* to the *ginásio*." Another man approaches me and asks (in Portuguese, spoken by all of these people) a revealing question: "What kind of service to us are you offering?" None, I say; I am here just to look around. "*Turista. Aqui,*" he says, and shakes his head in wonderment. Yet another man asks if I have any sort of *remédio* for his sick children. Everyone has bad teeth.

We poke into an *igarapé* to look at a *serra* or "mountain," which, we are told, is a principal tourist attraction. The stream is about fifty meters wide and is bordered by stunted trees as well as many tall and slender Assai palms emerging gracefully from the black water. A blindingly orange butterfly crosses from one side (bank is not a word that applies here) to the other, then a large lime-green dragonfly. Birds are scarce, but I glimpse a large, rusty-colored one bearing the ponderous name of *orependula*, as it too makes the rapid traverse. A large black dolphin or *boto*, a creature held in Amazonian tradition to be responsible, in some sort of anthropomorphic fashion, for all men's marital infidelities, surfaces near us. I shock the crew by announcing that in the States there is a species of *boto* that we eat. The *serra* is unimpressive, a rock no more than seven meters high, marking a right-angle curve in the stream. We turn around, ploughing our bow into the flooded forest in the process, and head back for the Uaupés.

This is the apex of our trip, for today we are due to meet Judith back in Trovão, a full afternoon's run downstream. We pass São Pedro and then pause for luncheon at the deserted nearby island. I swim from its sandy beach, and the water feels like the softest flannel. The others only bathe, soaping and scrubbing themselves with great enthusiasm but not swimming a stroke. I wonder if they know how. In most respects the crew is no less cleanly than the fastidious Indians, who every day spend much time washing themselves or their clothes. After lunch (consisting mostly of a broth made from a toothpick-legged chicken purchased in the morning and soon killed and plucked by Luís on his after-deck butcher's block), we resume our easy meander downstream. We make a brief second stop at Cunuri. 'Zé Maria buys seven live hens and a rooster and dumps them all into a large, loosely woven Indian basket. I buy a small, well-carved model of an Indian canoe. It is mounted on a round penholder. "The mission has us make them," the vendor tells me. Luís buys one too, for the same price of 5,000 cruzeiros.

The old Indian who first told us about the *doido* appears, still searching. He asks if we can tow his canoe down to the junction with the Rio Negro. We agree and he carefully makes his way aboard. He does not bring his gun or his machete. Faustino and the old man talk spiritedly as we set forth again. I leaf through some incongruous World Bank publications about colonization and development prospects in a far-off corner of Amazonia, and wonder whether such schemes could ever work along the Uaupés. Great individual creativity is evident here, but where is a sense of collective purpose sufficient to bring off grand designs? Who are the leaders, other than the missionaries on whom the Indians seem so largely to depend? If everybody wants to move to Manaus, what hope is there for the success of new colonies?

My train of thought is interrupted by a series of thumps. Soon we are hard aground. Faustino is furious with himself. "I wasn't paying attention," he says. "I was talking too much." The Indian stands on the bow and tries with a long pole to maneuver us toward deeper water. The rest of us hop into the thigh-deep river and push from the stern, which angles forward and down into the water from the bitter end. Faustino, strong and sinewy, gets under the incline and pushes up and forward with his shoulders. "*Um, dois, três,*" he grunts. Then we all shove. The boat moves a foot at a time. In between pushes, 'Zé Maria and Luís whoop and splash in the water like children.

After forty-five tiring minutes we are free. The motor, which has been strained during the process, has developed a worrisome new sound rather like that made by howler monkeys. At four-thirty we pull into Trovão. Judith should have arrived at three o'clock, but there is no sign of her. "The *doido* must be dead by now," someone says. Cumulus clouds build high into the sky, and their reflections decorate the still black water as the first hint of evening comes. A small boy and a young Indian man with a mutilated lip throw skipping stones across the water. I wonder if Judith got bumped from the Thursday plane as well. We decide to continue to the junction with the Rio Negro, knowing that we will see her boat if it comes, because traffic on the river is so light. She shows up half an hour later. The plane had been late and the usual "delays" had occurred in São Gabriel, even though Judith, spirited swiftly through town to the waiting boat by Vanduir, had been spared a trip to the dentist. We proceed to the house of Cesário da Lancha, the trader at São Joaquim, for the night. When we arrive the old Indian gathers his belongings, walks across a narrow and treacherous plank to the shore, and moves off to continue his quest.

Good geographer that she is, Judith has brought detailed maps of the region that she found in Manaus for a hundred cruzeiros apiece. We study them and discuss the problems of mapping Amazonia even with modern technology. One major effort, called Projecto Radam and launched in the mid-1970s, employs radar scanning. By studying the different colors on Radam maps, you can tell which parts of Amazonia are good for farming and which parts are inhospitable, but, Judith says, few people have ever actually gone out into the field to verify the radar interpretations, and they are often misleading. Another system, operating on the basis of remote sensing from the LANDSAT satellite, is more accurate but it cannot penetrate the clouds that almost always cover large portions of the basin. "The satellite's orbit varies in such a way that micro-regions are usually only surveyed once every few years," Judith explains. "If it happens to be cloudy that day, tough luck. For a lot of the basin, there is no LANDSAT data whatever."

Dinner aboard 'Zé Maria's *tolda*. In foreground: Judith Gunn, the cultural geographer *(Roger D. Stone)*

Although government planners have used the Radam and LANDSAT data to substantiate theories supporting the viability of big-league agricultural enterprises for Amazonia, Judith remains skeptical. Along with many natural scientists who work on Amazonian questions, she holds the view that its soils are far too acid, and too devoid of nutrients, for large-scale plantation farming or cattle ranching to be independently profitable in most parts of the basin. Dinner arrives—scrawny chicken again, even though temptingly fresh *paraíba* was bought this morning from an Indian canoe. Faustino's evening entertainment is a broadcast, in rapid-fire sportscaster Portuguese that is unintelligible to all but a few foreigners, of a soccer game between Brazil and Paraguay. We manage to catch that the game ends in a tie.

Friday, October 14

'Zé Maria and Faustino are up before dawn to carry about thirty lengths of sawn hardwood from Cesário's warehouse to the boat. Soon 'Zé Maria is going to replace his thatched *tolda* roof with a permanent wooden one ("It will be hotter but it will last longer"), and he will use Cesário's wood for the job. The wood is tossed onto the cabin floor. The basket of chickens emits feeble clucks. The rooster attempts to crow. Luís dispatches the creature, thus fulfilling the old Brazilian saying, "*Cala boca, ou vai na sopa*"—shut up, or you go into the soup pot.

Luís and Faustino hop aboard with breathless news. "The *doido* has been found," says 'Zé Maria. "He came down in a canoe from Trovão." "He wasn't *doido* at all," Faustino adds. "He didn't try to kill anybody and he recognized everybody, even 'Zé Maria." Neither 'Zé Maria nor Faustino could explain to me where he had been, or why. Several Indians, not including the old man, board a canoe and paddle off into the strangely foggy morning. Presumably the *doido* is one of them, but I cannot get a good look before the canoe disappears from view.

Soon after our own departure we reach the place where the Uaupés and the Rio Negro meet. Today our plan is to go up the Rio Negro as far as possible, then turn back in time to reach São Gabriel by nightfall. We stop at a nondescript village called Icatu, where 'Zé Maria does business with a mostly Indian trader who owns many goods but has no motorized boat. He wants to travel up the Içana River to sell his inventory to the gold prospectors, but the man who promised him a ride up has yet to appear. 'Zé Maria tries to sell him a new outboard motor for 500,000 cruzeiros. When this fails, 'Zé Maria suggests a used one for 300,000. There is no response, positive or negative, but 'Zé Maria has no doubt as to what has happened. "He doesn't have the money," he says, and we wander back to the boat. For lunch we ascend to a deserted place named Açai, after the handsome tall palm tree whose necklace-like strings of fruit produce everything from wine to a purplish ice cream, tasting vaguely of gritty black currant, that is much admired in Amazonia. Judith and I swim in the still flannel water and the crew washes, while parakeets roost and screech in the palm trees. This is the closest we will get to Humboldt's San Carlos, to the Orinoco river system that is so tantalizingly near, to the Cassiquiare River that Humbolt was probably the first European to identify as the link between the Orinoco and Amazon river systems.

View from the Rio Negro, near the mouth of the Uaupés. High mountains in the background are more typical of scenery around Rio de Janeiro than of gently rolling (or flat) Amazonia. *(Roger D. Stone)*

Soon after noon we begin the downstream sleigh ride through waters that flow more swiftly as we move closer to the narrows at São Gabriel. The sky turns gray, and light showers dapple the water. There are no settlements along here, only an occasional house in a clearing carved from the dense forest. Canoe traffic, though, is becoming heavier. In one vessel we see an Indian woman with a small, startlingly blond child. We arrive at São Gabriel on schedule, just before dark, in time to watch a trading boat from the town of Itacoatiara, near Manaus, take aboard a load of goods from a large flatbed truck that has been all but driven into the river to make the delivery. Eggs, a large freezer, several tricycles, and cooking oil all form part of the cargo.

It is raining slightly when Judith and I go ashore for dinner. We pass many houses with color television sets blazing. Aging national programs, it turns out, are being rebroadcast on a local closed-circuit system. It quickly became so popular, Vanduir tells us later, that it caused the closing of the town's only movie house. Judith, whose Ph.D. thesis project is an intensive survey of *caboclo* farming and eating habits along one primitive stretch of the Solimões, at the mouth of the Purus, is fascinated by what she sees in São Gabriel's bustling shops. "It's a different world," she says. "The people on 'my' island have hardly heard of some of these things. Most of them have never eaten some of the food available here, and most of them have never seen television *or* a movie." It is a twenty-two-hour passenger boat ride from where she lives to Manaus, Judith continues. Rather than make the trip to buy canned or dried foods and other staples, most people stay home and eat fish and manioc and whatever else they can grow or find locally.

At the restaurant where Vanduir lives, we continue to discuss the differences between the two rivers and their people. The Solimões is not "black" and barren like the Rio Negro, but "white" or, more accurately, the color of coffee heavily laced with cream. As it flows eastward it carries with it rich supplies of nutrients from the geologically recent Andes, where many of its tributaries begin. Along the alluvial floodplains, or *várzeas*, of the Solimões, conditions are therefore good for the planting of annual crops during the low-water seasons. Life is relatively abundant on the Solimões; mosquitoes are, for example, thick there—a characteristic that contrasts sharply with the virtually bug-free Rio Negro. "One slap at sunset and you'll kill half a dozen," Judith says. "To understand Amazonia you must understand its diversity."

Vanduir and others are loading chairs and tables aboard a large truck. "We're having a dance on the roof above the supermarket," he explains. "Last March we tried the same thing and it was a great success, so we are trying again." After dinner Judith and I walk past the supermarket, where a crowd has begun to form even though there is no music yet. Luís is there. He looks jumpy and eager. "I'm going to be up all night," he says. At least until the *cachaça* runs out, I think.

Saturday, October 15

Gray dawn after the rainy night. 'Zé Maria has gone home to his family, but Faustino is aboard. Luís snores quietly, rolled so tightly into his hammock that nothing can be seen of him but a vaguely tubelike outline. Judith and I go ashore for breakfast (bread!) and to have another look at São Gabriel's rapid lurch into the modern world. Morning traffic is heavy. The big flatbed truck and several *fuscas* splash down the commercial thoroughfare.

Back at the boat we find the whole crew. "I'm leaving for Colombia on Monday," says 'Zé Maria. "I'll be gone for two weeks. I have a lot to do to get ready." Faustino, seeming sentimental, says good-bye and finally leaves after several false starts. Judith asks 'Zé Maria if the boat has a name. "No," he says. "I thought maybe I'd just call it *São Gabriel*." I say, "How about *O Beijinho do Uaupés*?"—The Little Kiss of the Uaupés. "I like that," says 'Zé Maria. His face lights up in a quick small smile. He and Luís both go off to try to find Vanduir, who is to take me back to the airport. While they are gone, Vanduir shows up alone and we leave with him. We look for 'Ze Maria and Luís to say good-bye, but they have vanished.

Soon I am back in Manaus. At a travel agency an American woman stands forlornly before the counter. "Where," she demands, "is the opera house? The only reason I wanted to come to Manaus was to see the opera house, and now I can't even find the opera house and this morning's all the time we have left. You didn't even have the opera house on the list of things to do, and all I want to do is see it. You must tell me where it is."

The travel agent looks back impassively and says, "You want to come with me on the boat ride?"

In the hurly-burly of Manaus, where an economic boom has been created, thanks to a duty-free zone providing contrived bargains for visitors from southern Brazil, I reflect on the experience of the past few days. For one thing, it occurs to me, Judith and I have glimpsed a "traditional" Amazonia where there remains a relative balance between man and nature. Indians, *caboclos* like the sturdy Faustino, and "foreign" traders like 'Zé Maria all seem to function in a spirit of easy camaraderie and mutual respect. Each understands the other's role, and the system works. It could continue working, I think, unless the pressure of population were to force change—and the pace of change, too, seems inexorable. "São Gabriel is changing, and not for the better in my opinion," Margaret Mee had written me. Surely she is right. The color television, the fifteen taxis, the incipient sprawl of the commercial section already give it the appearance of a micro-Manaus. From São Gabriel one can envision outward ripples of heedless deforestation—for cattle ranches that will fail in the long run because of the poor soil, for timber, even for weekend country houses. Soon, as is now happening in Manaus, will come the time when to drink a cup of water from the Rio Negro will be to risk diarrhea, when fish will be even scarcer, when the already feeble Indians lingering in the river settlements will be reduced to full dependency upon a new system of which they can be expected to comprehend nothing.

Such is the outlook for São Gabriel, or so it seems, from the perspective of Manaus, for a place that Judith and I had thought would symbolize an enduring primitive wilderness, a living example of what all of Amazonia had once been. In this sense we, too, had been duped by a region that has always frustrated those who have developed hopes and dreams based upon it. From the old legend of El Dorado to tycoon D. K. Ludwig's quixotic recent lunge to grow rice and pulpwood along the Jari River, from hopes that the basin could be transformed into an Arcadia to the assumption that the region's nineteenth-century rubber boom would be the route to enduring prosperity, *Homo sapiens* has usually been the big loser in the Amazonian game. History and science both provide ample documentation of what happened and why. But we are a weed species, as the sage S. Dillon Ripley of the Smithsonian Institution has put it, and we continue to press forward, with improved technology and maddening determination, with efforts to transform the Center of the Earth into merely another mediocre part of it.

CHAPTER 2

Early Times

A BILLION YEARS AGO, IN LATE PRECAMBRIAN TIMES, THERE WAS NO SOUTH America. The entire world was still a single landmass, now called Pangaea. As the planet took shape, there were widespread glaciations. The seas advanced and retreated. Life consisted largely of bacteria and algae. In what was to become Amazonia, the highest points of land became the so-called Brazilian and Guianan "shields." These were two massifs of very old gneissic and granitic rock that formed an eastward-pointing V flanking Amazonia to the north and south and joining near what is now Santarém. In the absence of the Andes, still only modest foldings when Pangaea began to break into northern and southern sections during the late Paleozoic era, about 280 million years ago, Amazonia was a vast inland sea opening to the Pacific. The basin had no eastern mouth since Africa, too, was part of Gondwana, as the southern portion of Pangaea is now called. Perhaps 150 million years ago, South America began to drift westward away from Africa, and the Atlantic Ocean was born. As the Andes gradually rose, the former sea became a large freshwater lake. Only very recently, perhaps two to four million years ago, the Andes as we now know them came into being with a series of mighty upthrusting heaves of the earth.

Then, at last, the waters punched through the low, softening hills at the juncture of the two "shields" and began to flow eastward into the Atlantic. At this time—during the Quaternary period of the Cenozoic (most recent) geological era—the region finally achieved the fundamental shape that remains today.

During these long epochs of inundation, the floor of the basin was being covered by thickening layers of sand and sediment eroded and weathered away from the ancient massifs. These deposits, never rich in nutrients in the first

Another example, from Alfred Russel Wallace's book, of how the Amazonian forest was perceived by nineteenth-century explorers

place, were further leached by rainfall during their slow progress down the slopes and into the waters. There, accumulating steadily from the very outset of geologic time, they reached depths of up to more than three kilometers. These are the barren soils of what is known as the *terra firme*, poor in inorganic nutrients, that still cover almost all of Amazonia except for about two percent of the region lying along the riverbanks. In these floodplain or *várzea* areas, annual doses of minerals and other nutrients wash down from the weathering crust of the far younger Andes during the flood seasons. Agricultural conditions in the *várzea* are even better than they were in the highly fertile Nile Valley before the Aswan High Dam halted its annual cycle, since the Amazon's different rhythm allows more time for harvesting and drainage. Elsewhere in Amazonia, though, the very elements that sustain life had largely been lost from the ancient soils through leaching before plants had even begun to grow there.

During these prehistoric ages, millions of years ago, the great Amazonian forest or *hylaea*, as Humboldt termed it from the composite Greek for a rainy wooded area, was already in place. In such a forest, tall trees with slender, smooth trunks drive straight for the sky, then explode into sudden crowns of branches bearing dark green elliptical leaves that help form the lofty canopy. These trees occur in twentyfold the number of species that are to be found in temperate forests; to identify a "sterile" one that is neither fruiting nor in bloom is often a challenge even for professionals. Typically they have small nondescript flowers that in some species emerge not from branches but straight from the trunk. The trees do not stand alone; almost invariably they are garlanded with a glorious tangle of climbing plants and other epiphytes such as bromeliads (members of the pineapple family) and many species of orchid. Smaller plants and shrubs forming lower layers of the multitiered forest compete for the scant light that penetrates the canopy. The floor of this forest consists not of tangled "jungle," which can only occur where there is more light, but of a thin layer of brown, fast-decomposing leaf litter covering the moist soil. To walk through it you no more require a machete than you would to walk through a temperate evergreen forest. Your feet are likely to get wetter, though, for it is never dry underfoot in an untouched piece of Amazonian *hylaea*.

Four times during the Pleistocene era, which began 1.6 million years ago, ice pushed across the face of the earth, at one stage covering as much as 27 percent of its surface and reaching a depth of as much as 3,500 meters. Amazonia became unstable during this period. First, arid stretches when no rain fell caused much of the tropical forest, which had largely come into being some fifty million years earlier, to turn into sparsely vegetated open plains. Later came the effects of ice, melting during the late Pleistocene from a cap covering the Andes and from glaciers reaching down toward the lowlands.

The result was centuries of inundation, when water levels rose from deep riverbeds in much of the middle and lower Amazon basin and immersed all but small portions of the forest. During the drier phases, according to the zoologist P. E. Vanzolini of the University of São Paulo, the Amazonian forest was reduced to "isolated patches," or refuges where "populations were isolated and consequently became differentiated." During wetter periods, ranges were extended and formerly isolated populations intermingled. Vanzolini and other scientists, notably the ornithologist Jurgen Haffer, who published a benchmark article on the subject in 1969, have come to believe that these Pleistocene cycles of wetness and dryness are the primary reason why Amazonia has achieved such a remarkable degree of biological diversity.

Opinions vary on this subject, as we shall see in Chapter 6. However it happened, it is worth underscoring here that Amazonia has come to contain more species than any other place on earth. There are 2,500 different kinds of fish, 50,000 higher plant species, a countless number of invertebrates. In all, perhaps 10 percent of the world's five to ten million species of living things are to be found in Amazonia. Many are endemic to the region—that is, they cannot be found elsewhere. Discoveries of new forms of life have always been commonplace in Amazonia, and they remain so. In 1982, a new plant species was found right on the small campus of Brazil's National Amazon Research Institute, on the outskirts of Manaus. According to one estimate, 85 percent of all the species in Amazonia remain undiscovered.

As noteworthy as the basin's complex ecology is its immense size, a characteristic that almost always gets top billing in the literature of Amazonia. In all, the Amazon River watershed boasts an area of some 7.8 million square kilometers, sprawling across no fewer than eight South American nations: Bolivia, Brazil, Colombia, Ecuador, Guyana, Peru, Suriname, and Venezuela. The region is about as large as Europe including the Soviet Union west of the Urals. Five million square kilometers of Amazonia constitute Brazil's "legal Amazonia," which in turn represents fully 57 percent of all Brazil (this is the standard geographical unit referred to in this volume unless specifically noted otherwise). A second definition limits Brazilian Amazonia to its "geographic" or "classic" proportions, encompassing some 3.5 million square kilometers and about 42 percent of Brazilian territory. The purpose of this narrower limit is to omit pre-Amazonian savanna or border lands, and include only the portions of the region that are dominated by moist tropical forest. But even within the smaller zone there are many different kinds of forest. One scientist, Dr. Keith Brown of the University of Campinas in Brazil's state of São Paulo, has estimated that real tropical forest (very narrowly defined) covers not the 95 percent of the basin that is often suggested, but only around 40 percent.

The Amazon tumbles swiftly eastward from its source, usually said to be the Lago Lauricocha, which lies some 150 kilometers from the Pacific Ocean and 4,000 meters up in the Peruvian Andes. Spaniards call the river the Marañón until it reaches the Brazilian border at Tabatinga, where its name becomes the Solimões. Two substantial rivers, the Napo and the Ucayali, join the Marañón before it even reaches the border; between there and Manaus the Solimões merges with other large rivers—the Putumayo, the Japurá, the Juruá, the Purus—and many smaller tributaries, of which there are no fewer than 1,100 in the entire system. Near the Encontro das Águas, close to Manaus, where the Rio Negro joins it from the northwest, the Solimões is so wide that you can hardly see one bank from the other. Below Manaus, the scope of the river, now truly the majestic Amazon, becomes even more impressive as it flows toward the Atlantic in a stately gradient. While the river channel remains relatively narrow, the extent of the *várzea* doubles to about fifty kilometers east of Manaus, and attains its maximum width of some 330 kilometers at the formidable delta near Belém. Once fully combined, the "white" Solimões and the "black" Rio Negro form an Amazon yellow-ochre in color, still relatively rich in suspended Andean nutrients, and seventy meters deep at the Óbidos Narrows, near Santarém. Some 6,700 kilometers long, the Amazon barely outranks the Nile as the world's longest river. Its drainage area is two and a half times as big, though, and its basin contains 20 percent of all the world's river water. Just one of its mouths disgorges into the Atlantic Ocean an impressive 255,000 cubic meters per second; the system's total discharge is estimated as being four times greater than that of the Zaire (Congo), the world's second largest, and eleven times that of the Mississippi. It is hard to argue that the Amazon is not the world's most formidable body of fresh water.

This was the huge and watery and abundant environment that, as the Pleistocene ended, began to welcome yet another new species: the human being. Fleeing from the advancing ice cap, man crossed the Bering land bridge and entered the New World some thirty thousand years ago. Perhaps as early as 2000 B.C., when the ancient Egyptian civilization was already far advanced, the first human beings made their way into the Amazonian lowlands. Some may have entered via the Antilles from Florida, and some may have crossed from the Colombian highlands. The most traveled route was probably down from the Andean heights at the western end of the basin. For these early colonists, Amazonia stood out in welcome contrast to the rigors of the cold and empty highlands. Although the large mammals upon which many primitive people depended were in short supply, they encountered an abundance of plant and animal life. Among the luxuriant array of plants that covered the barren forest floor were many that man could either eat or put to other uses. Fish, manatees, and giant turtles abounded in the waters and were easily captured. In the trees were primates and large birds.

What use the aboriginal Amazonians made of these resources has, until recent years, been largely a matter of conjecture. Few archaeologists have been

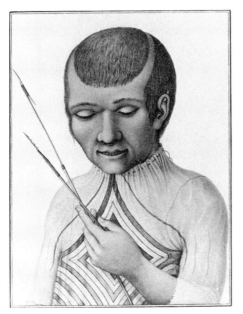

Illustrations of Amazonian Indians from Alexandre Rodrigues Ferreira's classic *Viagem Filosófica*

attracted to the region; the obstacles they traditionally cite include constantly shifting river channels that may have obliterated many ancient settlements, and thick vegetation that may conceal remaining ones even from the probing gaze of modern satellites. For lack even of pebbles in some parts of Amazonia, after hundreds of millions of years of constant erosion, tools and other artifacts were made of wood and other perishable materials. The earliest carbon-dated record of man within Amazonia is no older than 980 B.C., though there is evidence of coastal occupation from one thousand years before. For all these reasons, it was long thought that before its "discovery," Amazonia was occupied by small numbers of quite primitive aborigines.

Recent archaeological evidence, though, has caused quite a sharp reversal in how early human life in Amazonia is now perceived. Stone tools, jade ornaments, and "scads of pottery," reports Anna Curtenius Roosevelt of the Museum of the American Indian in New York City, have lately been found in sites not only near the coast, but along floodplains throughout the basin. Some of the sites are large and are known to have been constantly occupied for thousands of years. Although some were probably hunter-gatherers, many of Amazonia's earliest settlers began practicing there the "slash and burn" techniques of shifting agriculture that are commonplace in all tropical forest regions. The need for large amounts of land to sustain this type of farming tended to keep individual villages small in size, with usual populations of perhaps 150 to 200. Some communities achieved populations in the thousands, however, and the fertile *várzea* regions could support many settlements that large. After years of careful analysis, the biogeographer William Denevan in 1977 issued an upward revision of his own earlier data. The aboriginal Amazonian population of what is now modern Brazil, he calculated, numbered at least 3.6 million people and perhaps as many as 4,834,000. By the fifteenth century A.D., in other words, the basin may have been supporting a relatively sophisticated population as large as at any subsequent time up to the 1970s. Since the island of Hispaniola had a native population estimated at 250,000 when Christopher Columbus colonized it in 1496, Denevan's count for all of Brazilian Amazonia hardly seems exaggerated.

In his exhaustive doctoral thesis, entitled *A Rich Realm of Nature Destroyed: The Middle Amazon Valley, 1640–1750*, the historian David Graham Sweet thus describes life along the Solimões at the time of the first European arrivals in the sixteenth century:

> The horticulture of the Solimões peoples produced bitter and sweet manioc, corn, squash, sweet potatoes, peppers, peanuts, pineapples and a variety of tree fruits which may have come from cultivated orchards.... Among wild animals used for food were the turtle, manatee, fish, parrots, monkeys, iguanas, tapir, wild pigs and deer. Among the more remarkable technologies for food

The monkey, the manatee (below), and the peccary (opposite): three Amazonian species commonly eaten by aboriginal peoples, and depicted here by Rodrigues Ferreira's artists

gathering were the collection of great numbers of river turtles kept in pens to provide meat during flood seasons, and the preservation of fish and meat by smoking and drying in the absence of salt. Food was produced in remarkable quantities, with surpluses readily available for feeding visitors or for trade. There was a well-developed artisanry: pottery (including the production of pots of extraordinary size, and of a great variety of domestic utensils), spinning, weaving and drying of cloth made from domestically grown cotton. These products, as well as manioc bread, dried fish and feathers, were traded with people living inland. At least some people wore ornaments crafted in gold which was obtained by trade. Alcoholic beverages were produced by fermentation, and sometimes consumed to the point of drunkenness. The men were very skillful in manufacturing and handling dugout canoes of all sizes, commonly made of great trunks captured as they floated past during flood season.

For native Amazonians, the arrival of the Europeans resulted in little other than disease, destruction, decimation, and slavery. Whether they were *conquistadores*, traders, or soldiers, few of the Spanish and Portuguese adventurers who began to penetrate the basin starting in the early sixteenth century seemed interested in trying to understand the environment in which they found themselves, or the people their weapons enabled them to dominate. Not until Jesuits and other missionaries made their appearance did any Europeans manifest any interest in the welfare of the Amazonian aborigines. Even the churchmen, as we shall see, had their own reasons to offer them protection. The rest of those

Another traditional source of food (for meat and eggs) was the freshwater turtle, thought by European explorers to have been hunted with bows and arrows
(top) and eviscerated on the beaches. The illustration below also comes from
Viagem Filosófica.

who arrived were truly misfits. They were looking not for tropical forests, but for India and for gold. Their skills were maritime, military, and mercantile; few were trained to found colonies or farms. Yet, in a sense, it is their very unpreparedness for life near and in Amazonia that gives them important, if only occasionally admirable, roles in our story.

In all probability, though there are other theories, it was none other than Christopher Columbus who led the way toward the European discovery of Amazonia. In 1498 this skilled and determined navigator set out on the third of his four voyages to the Americas, once again commissioned by Their Catholic Highnesses King Ferdinand and Queen Isabella of Castile. One of this trip's purposes was to provision the colony that Columbus had already founded in Hispaniola (Haiti). Another was to continue the frustrating search for the elusive passage from the Caribbean to the fabled Indies, this time by means of an effort to find the great continent thought by some (prominently including Dom João II of Portugal) to lie south or southeast of the Antilles. On July 31, Columbus's fleet sighted the high Trinity Hills at the southeast corner of the island of Trinidad. According to the spirited and detailed account compiled by Samuel Eliot Morison in his classic *The European Discovery of America*, the admiral then closed with the shore and proceeded westward along Trinidad's southern coast. Rounding Punta Arenal at the island's southwestern tip, he ordered his fleet to anchor for a few days' rest. "His only contact with the natives at this point was mildly comic," wrote Morison. "He had been hoping to encounter either Chinese mandarins or black potentates like those on the Gold Coast. But when a dugout canoe approached, he observed with disgust that it contained only naked Indians looking very like Caribs."

Perhaps because the people looked so familiar, Columbus was slow to realize that he was fast closing on the continent he had been commissioned to find. But only days after his first exploration of Trinidad he crossed the Gulf of Paria and anchored. Greeted only by monkeys, he waded ashore to become part of the first group of Europeans ever to set foot on the South American continent. For some days he held to his original belief that what is now known as the Paria Peninsula in modern Venezuela was yet another Caribbean island. As he continued westward, however, he noted fresh water flowing out of several river mouths and extending well out to sea. "I believe that this is a very great continent, until today unknown," he conceded in his journal after a full fortnight of exploration. "And if this be a continent, it is a marvelous thing, and will be so among all the wise, since so great a river flows that it makes a freshwater sea of forty-eight leagues." Columbus guessed right; the river of which he wrote was the Orinoco.

Less than a year after Columbus's momentous discovery, another expedition left Spain for the New World. It was led by Alonso de Ojeda, a veteran of Columbus's second voyage, and by the Florentine merchant Amerigo Vespucci, who commanded two of the expedition's four ships. Described by Morison as "courageous, ruthless, greedy and exceptionally cruel," Ojeda had studied the notes and charts from Columbus's third voyage. He decided to try his hand along the same coast in search of pearls (of which Columbus had gathered a few), found financial support, and set off in 1499. Through a miscalculation in navigation the Ojeda fleet made its landfall somewhere in the Guianas, then turned westward. Although the crew noted sweet water as the ships passed the mouths of the Orinoco, Ojeda made no effort to explore them. Instead he proceeded on a clockwise tour of the southern Caribbean that included visits to the Paria Peninsula and to Lake Maracaibo.

In 1500, Ojeda returned to Spain with a few pearls and with Indians he had taken as slaves despite stern warnings from Ferdinand and Isabella against mistreating the natives. Ojeda was never to return to the South American continent. The significance of his voyage, in fact, lies largely in the part in it that Vespucci may have played. What is truth and what is fantasy in the writings of the colorful Florentine, the only person in history for whom two continents are named, has puzzled scholars for centuries. His outlandish claim that on one of his voyages he had sailed northwest from the Caribbean across the continental United States to Vancouver, British Columbia, casts doubt even on more modest assertions. One of these, presented as fact in Edward J. Goodman's detailed volume *The Explorers of South America*, was that Vespucci was in fact the policymaker of the Ojeda expedition. Far more interested in finding the passage to India than in pearls and slaves, Vespucci claims to have separated from Ojeda near the coast and proceeded in a southeasterly direction in search of a mythical "cape" long thought to have represented the eastern doorway to the Indian Ocean.

On July 2, 1499, about a month after leaving Ojeda, Vespucci asserts, he found himself entering a "wide gulf" that may have been the estuary leading to the Amazon. For four days his ships continued upstream, finding no place to land. He then anchored, Vespucci continued, and rowed for four more days. As had Columbus at Paria, Vespucci eventually concluded that what he had discovered was not the route to India but a large intervening landmass. Enthused as he and his men were at the beauty of the landscape, Vespucci therefore returned to the open sea and continued southeasterly until an unfavorable current forced him to give up the search for the fabled passage and reverse course to rejoin Ojeda at Hispaniola.

Columbus had, then, sensed great volumes of fresh water flowing from the South American continent. Ojeda and perhaps Vespucci had confirmed the notion. Soon afterward came the first real penetration of the Amazon by Vicente Yáñez Pinzón, a seasoned navigator who had skippered the *Niña* on the first Columbus voyage. Pinzón, like Ojeda, had managed to get a look at Columbus's accounts of his survey of the "pearl coast." Funding for a new look followed with relative ease because Columbus's credibility had worn thin among Spaniards disenchanted by his inability to produce treasures from India. With a fleet of four vessels, Pinzón set forth late in 1499 on a course that was deliberately more southerly than that followed by previous expeditions. In January 1500, Pinzón made a landfall somewhere along the coast of northern Brazil—conjecture varies as to exactly where—and turned west and north toward Trinidad and the Paria Peninsula.

While far out to sea, well out of sight of land, Pinzón noted the freshness of the water at one point, and decided to veer south to investigate. Although he later wrote that he had been sailing near the Ganges, what he had in fact discovered was one of the many mouths of the Amazon. He proceeded some eighty kilometers upriver and encountered friendly Indians, of whom he captured thirty-six. The discovery turns out to have been the high point of the Pinzón voyage. What ensued, as he continued past the Paria Peninsula on the customary clockwise route, was a series of battles, shipwrecks, losses of lives, and—finally—a tattered return to Spain. At least, however, Pinzón had managed to arrive in Amazonia a few weeks before another Spaniard, Diego de Lepe, entered the river (which he named the Marañón) and killed many Indians. Although Lepe was the first of the two to arrive back in Spain, and for a while was given credit for the European discovery of the great river, the distinction must clearly be awarded to Pinzón. Lepe was not forgotten, however; to this day the Peruvian Amazon bears the name Marañón.

Although he made what was probably the first landfall along the Brazilian coast, Pinzón is not generally conceded to have been Brazil's European discoverer. The accolade is more usually awarded to the Portuguese navigator Pedro Álvares Cabral, a linear descendant of widening circles of Portuguese maritime exploration that began as early as 1420 with Prince Henry the Navigator and the discovery and colonization of Madeira. Throughout the fifteenth century the Portuguese pushed ever farther offshore and down the west coast of Africa. Bartolomeu Dias was, in this voyage of 1487–88, the first European to round the Cape of Good Hope; ten years later Vasco da Gama extended Portugal's range to Calicut (Calcutta) on the Malabar Coast, center of the spice trade previously carried out entirely by land. Da Gama returned exhausted to Portugal in 1499. Aware of the need to follow up quickly upon his success, he encouraged Cabral, a nobleman with little known nautical experience, to undertake a second voyage to Calicut.

Cabral closely followed da Gama's remarkably accurate instructions for rounding the Cape in the most efficient manner. They called for a wide swing west of the equatorial doldrums on a track that would take the fullest possible advantage of the trade winds. Any navigator, closely following da Gama's instructions, would cause his vessel to pass near the easternmost bulge of Brazil, near Recife. Only a slight bit of drift to starboard was required for an actual landfall. On April 22, 1500, one of the lookouts in Cabral's fleet spotted a mountain to the west. The captain altered course to close with the shore, and thus became the first European to reach Brazil south of Amazonia. Cabral and his fleet spent eight days in a harbor, about halfway between Recife and Rio de Janeiro, that he called Porto Seguro. They took on water and enjoyed friendly relations with local Tupi Indians, then pushed on for the destination of real importance to them: India. Cabral took little interest in Brazil, guessing that it was merely an island. But his achievement, far more than Pinzón's, triggered subsequent events. "It does not seem improper to maintain," wrote the historian Edward J. Goodman, "that he must be counted as the *effective* discoverer of Brazil."

Why did the Spaniards avoid what is now Brazil, and instead generally sail toward the Caribbean at the end of the fifteenth century? Why, despite the remarkable set of achievements posted by Spanish navigators beginning with Columbus, was it Cabral and not a Spaniard who achieved Brazil's "effective" discovery? The answer begins with the Treaty of Tordesillas, negotiated by Pope Alexander VI in 1494, that in effect divided the world between Spain and Portugal. Earlier in the fifteenth century, papal policies favoring Portugal over Spain had helped enable the Portuguese to become established along the West African coast and on the offshore islands. In 1492, however, the installation of a new pro-Spanish Pope coincided with Columbus's triumphant return, and led to renewed debate over which country would receive holy rights to which lands overseas. What eventually resulted was Tordesillas, which gave Spain all lands to the west of a north-south line 370 leagues west of the Cape Verde Islands, and awarded to Portugal everything to the east of that line. Portugal got India, Africa, and the Atlantic islands; Spain won the New World.

Who was to own Brazil, which remained undiscovered, later became a disputed matter, since the treaty did not specify whether the line's starting point was to be at the eastern or the western end of the Cape Verde chain. The most favorable interpretation for Portugal accorded her the right to no more than the bulge of Brazil—the land lying to the east of a line from just west of Belém to just west of São Paulo. A more stringent judgment would have granted Portugal only a grim little triangle consisting mostly of arid semidesert; Spain would have won Rio de Janeiro, São Paulo, and almost all of Amazonia. A bitter struggle might have erupted over the question but for the timely union of the two courts by wedlock. Ferdinand and Isabella had blessed the marriage of Dom Manuel "the fortunate" (successor to Dom João II) to their daughter Doña Isabel, Infanta of Castile, and after her death to their younger daughter, Doña María. They referred to the King of Portugal as "our son." Because of these ties, Spain's navigators were cautioned, over many years, against treading on Portuguese toes. Thus it was that, while the

Portuguese in the early sixteenth century sought little more in the New World than to retain their foothold in Brazil, the Spaniards were consolidating their position in the western Caribbean and advancing toward the Andes as well as into Mexico.

The story might have ended very differently. Before approaching the Spaniards, Columbus had solicited backing from Dom João II (great-nephew of Prince Henry the Navigator) for his scheme to sail west in search of a new route to India and the East. The irony of Dom João's denunciation of the proposal as "idiocy" was that Portugal consequently ended up in possession

Captain Francisco de Orellana

of Brazil. Spain, in the meantime, vigorously pursued the more northerly course that Columbus had charted with the backing of Ferdinand and Isabella. By 1513 Balboa reached the Pacific. Six years later a Spanish colony was established in Panama. This was Francisco Pizarro's jumping-off point for Peru, on whose shores he landed with some two hundred men in 1531. Exploiting internal dissent, he toppled the Incas in short order, established a capital at Lima, and began to exercise hegemony across Ecuador and into Colombia. Pizarro awarded his brother Gonzalo the regional command at Quito, and gave him instructions to probe eastward in search of the cinnamon and other spices that were in great demand as medicines and alleged to be plentiful there. The fabled El Dorado, a mythical Nirvana allegedly ruled by a king clad in gold dust, was also said to lie somewhere to the east. Installed as governor in December 1540, Gonzalo Pizarro hurriedly mounted an expeditionary force of 220 Spaniards and close to four thousand Indians. This clumsy band left Quito toward the end of February 1541 and began moving eastward across cold, mountainous, heavily forested, and altogether inhospitable terrain.

Captain Francisco de Orellana, another *conquistador* who had already participated in several chapters of the Peruvian conquest, was based at the coastal port of Guayaquil when he heard of the Gonzalo Pizarro mission. Orellana made haste to sign up and, with twenty-three men, joined Pizarro as lieutenant-general at his rain-drenched camp in Zumaco, about 160 kilometers east of Quito, after a miserable trip marked by hunger and Indian attacks. The united force faced many equally harrowing setbacks as it continued its eastward journey, encountering no gold and only occasional cinnamon trees. These, like most Amazonian plants, do not grow in the sorts of groves that Pizarro envisioned, but are loosely scattered across the forest and difficult to exploit commercially. Pizarro became so enraged by the Indians' inability to tell him where to find gold and spice trees that he ordered some burned, others torn apart by dogs. Food became scarce after all five thousand swine brought from Quito had been consumed and after other supplies were jettisoned because of the intense cold. As the Indians began to succumb to diseases and other ailments of the lower altitudes, and became vastly reduced in numbers from the four thousand who had begun the journey, it became necessary for Pizarro's men to build a "brigantine" to carry supplies and sick men along the river. Horses and men, still hopeful of finding El Dorado, followed on the riverbanks.

Pizarro pushed on until, according to his own reckoning, he was informed by guides that there lay ahead "a great uninhabited region in which there was no food whatsoever to be had," and accordingly halted the expedition to gather supplies. At this fateful moment Orellana, who had initially opposed the construction of the brigantine, now offered to forage ahead for food aboard the vessel and promised to return within twelve days. Pizarro accepted. In January

1542, almost a year after the expedition's departure from Quito, Orellana set forth with fifty-seven men, three arquebuses, and four or five crossbows.

Within several days of travel on the swift river (known to modern geographers as the Napo), Orellana and his crew had still not discovered food. They were reduced to eating hides, straps, and herb-flavored shoe soles. *In extremis*, they reached a friendly Indian village they called Aparia. After gaining strength there, Orellana considered a return voyage to Pizarro's camp. But according to his chronicler, Friar Gaspar de Carvajal, Orellana was dissuaded by dissenting comrades, who presented a petition to him. Soon he came himself to believe that "in no other way except down the river can our lives be saved." So Orellana left a fuming Pizarro (who eventually, if barely, made it back to Quito), and continued downstream after remaining in Aparia two months and building a second substantial vessel there.

Carvajal, appointed as "scrivener" by Orellana as protection against possible future charges against him in Madrid, reports a thrill-packed series of adventures as the party proceeded downstream. Orellana and his men once again faced hunger, as well as fierce attacks from a group of Indians they called the "Machiparo." Toward the end of June 1542, says Carvajal, the party reached "the excellent land and dominion of the Amazons," a rich and female-dominated society fashioned partly from Greek myth and partly from tales they had heard upriver. "We ourselves saw these women," a breathless Carvajal reports. They are "very white and tall and have hair very long and braided and wound about the head, and they are very robust and go about naked, with their privy parts covered, with their bows and arrows in their hands, doing as much fighting as ten Indian men, and indeed there was one woman among these who shot an arrow a span deep into one of the brigantines, and others less deep, so that our brigantines looked like porcupines." There were many other battles with Indians, of which one took place while half the crew was busy trying to fix one of the boats that had been stove in and swamped by a passing log.

At last, as Orellana and his men continued sailing downriver, they began to experience a considerable tide and dared hope that the ocean was near. The villages they passed contained unarmed Indians characterized by Carvajal as "a very docile people...of great intelligence, skillful in carving, drawing, and painting in all colors, very bright, such that it is a marvelous thing to see." On August 26, Orellana emerged from the river and turned westward, reaching harbor at the island of Cubagua. The captain returned from there to Spain to deliver his momentous news and seek support for a new expedition. This he obtained, returning as governor-general in 1550. The second voyage was, however, an utter failure. Orellana died of malaria during the course of it, while seeking entrance to the Amazon near the island of Marajó. His name lives on, though, as the first white man to have made the full journey down the river and to have fought with the Indians along its banks. His inadvertent adventure, moreover, launched a new era of exploration and conflict. Ironically, though, the principal beneficiary was to be Portugal.

CHAPTER 3

Exploring the Basin

ONE MIGHT HAVE THOUGHT THAT ORELLANA'S INADVERTENT ACCOMplishment would have triggered a wave of exploration as powerful as the tide that followed Columbus to the New World. But Spain hardly stirred. Under Tordesillas the lower Amazon was considered to be Portuguese territory, and early in the sixteenth century the two nations continued to be jointly ruled. The Pizarros and other prominent Spaniards in Peru were sufficiently preoccupied by bloody strife there to have little time left over for further cinnamon searches. Gold was abundant, and greed for it often resulted in sudden death in high places. By the mid-1550s, Gonzalo Pizarro had lost his head, his brother Francisco had been killed in battle, and Peru was being ruled by a new viceroy, Andrés Hurtado de Mendoza, who cared little for Amazonia. But Caryl P. Haskins, in his thorough geopolitical history entitled *The Amazon*, says that he favored a "general policy of promoting exploration, primarily to divert the attention of potential rebels from affairs at home."

As one result of this policy, Don Pedro de Ursúa, a former governor of Bogotá, was commissioned to mount a new expedition to look again for El Dorado and revisit the "Omágua" people who inhabited Orellana's "Aparia."

Ursuá's entourage included his fiancée, Doña Inés, as well as five maids, several hundred men, and horses and cattle. Ponderously this juggernaut made its way down the eastern slope of the Andes via the Huallaga and the Marañón. For the most part, these Spaniards kept themselves provisioned simply by stealing food and equipment from successive groups of Indians—the Omágua and then the Machiparos with whom Orellana had also been in contact—and slaughtering countless numbers of them. They were hardly less considerate of each other. Ursuá himself was stabbed to death by associates of a mutineer, friendless among historians, named Lope de Aguirre. His gang of pirates, which called itself the *Marañones*, took effective control of the expedition as it continued downriver, leaving a train of bloodshed, treachery, and inhuman treatment of Indians.

Opinion varies as to whether Aguirre followed Orellana to the Amazon's mouth and debouched by sailing past Marajó Island, or whether he was the first European to discover the Cassiquiare River in what is now southern Venezuela—the link between the Rio Negro and the Orinoco. The former is more likely. By whichever route, Aguirre and his crew reached open sea on July 1, 1561, and headed for Margarita Island, off the coast of Venezuela. "God only knows how we escaped out of that fearful lake," said Aguirre, who called himself "the Wanderer" and declared himself to be a rebel in a letter he later sent to King Philip of Spain. Soon afterward he was killed in battle, probably by his own men. If his end was no great loss, he had at least achieved another major feat of exploration. It was not to be duplicated until well into the seventeenth century, although many visits to the upper Marañón took place during the early 1600s, and some small settlements were established. Jesuit missions were founded in the region as early as 1638.

Although Portuguese traders had been engaging in lucrative slaving along the Guinea coast of West Africa since 1441, and must have considered the possibility of similar ventures in Amazonia, Portuguese colonists in Brazil were almost as hesitant as the Spaniards to move into the basin. Between 1534 and 1536, King João III divided the entire Brazilian coast into fourteen hereditary captaincies; from Santos in the south to Recife, which faces Africa at the easternmost point of the northeast, casual trading led to the establishment of small colonies. The Portuguese failed to round the bend to the north coast and the mouth of the river, however, thus leaving the way open for pioneers from other lands to begin the flow of the basin's resources to European markets. In search of such products as cinnamon, cocoa, aromatic roots, and oil seeds, the Dutch built small trading posts along the Xingu, a clear-water river flowing into the Amazon from the south. Although Walter Raleigh lost his head in 1618 as a consequence of his struggle to generate British interest in the search for El Dorado, the British, too, made several timid efforts to found colonies near the river's mouth. In 1612 an elegant French garrison landed on the island of Marañón (Maranhão) on the north coast and began the construction there of what is currently the bustling city of São Luís.

This direct challenge finally goaded the Portuguese into action. In 1615 they attacked and captured São Luís. From this forward base a further expedition to the mouth of the Amazon, led by Francisco Caldeira de Castello-Branco and including Captain Pedro de Teixeira, of whom we shall hear more, was mounted. The result was the founding, in 1619, of the fortified settlement of Nossa Senhora de Belém. In response to the newly aggressive Portuguese behavior, the Dutch simply moved to the south and east, entrenching themselves in a large region near Recife, where they remained until 1661, when the Portuguese bought them out, thus ending their occupancy of Brazilian territory. By as early as 1630, though, the Portuguese had put an end to all Dutch and English colonies in lower Amazonia, and established themselves as the dominant, permanent presence there.

Little by little, during the early seventeenth century, missionaries and adventurers moved eastward from the Andes to establish small settlements and missions. Zealous Franciscan priests were particularly active in the western headwaters. In 1636 two Franciscan monks, Domingo de Brieba and Andrés de Toledo, set out from Quito with a large expedition and reached a small settlement called Ante on the Aguarico River, near its junction with the Napo. Fortunate in being away from the encampment during a massacre carried out by local Indians, they decided or were persuaded by the circumstances to proceed downstream rather than attempt to make their way back to Quito. Just how they did it is unclear, but somehow Brieba and Toledo arrived at Pará late in 1637 after a grueling and lengthy voyage by canoe with only a small crew and none of the cumbersome logistical support that had characterized previous efforts. They thus became the first white men to complete the journey at least since the time of the scoundrel Lope de Aguirre (eighty years before), if not since Orellana.

The dramatic arrival of the two Spanish monks once again prompted a Portuguese reaction: the first full-fledged expedition up the river ever to be mounted. It was organized in July 1637 by Governor Fernando Noronha of Pará and led by the same Captain Pedro de Teixeira who had helped to capture São Luís from the Dutch and to found Belém. Brieba, the Franciscan, served as guide. In 1920 the Reverend George Edmundson, a Scotsman, presented a paper on the subject to the Royal Historical Society in London. With awe he noted that forty-seven large canoes to be manned by seventy white soldiers had been assembled, and that the supporting cast consisted of some 1,200 Indian men and women.

For a single vessel carrying but a small number of persons to drift downstream for some 3,500 miles was so fraught with difficulties and dangers that its

successful accomplishment was ascribed to the intervention of a special prov-
idence by the imagination of wondering contemporaries. But the task set
before Teixeira of conducting so large a fleet upstream against the current by
force of rowing and to obtain the supplies absolutely necessary for the feeding
of some 1,500 persons might well have appeared insuperable. That Teixeira
not only arrived at Quito, but that he brought his expedition safely back to
Pará, makes this double voyage of his, as a mere feat of human skill and
endurance, quite apart from its great value, historically and geographically,
worthy of special record.

Teixeira's arrival in Quito in 1638, after a ten-month voyage, provoked
apprehension among the Spaniards. Although Spain and Portugal continued
to be ruled jointly by Philip IV of Spain, the Tordesillas Treaty also remained
in effect. The Teixeira expedition suggested (accurately, as it turned out) a
worrisome burst of Portuguese interest in dominating the basin well to the
west of the famous line of demarcation. Quito consulted with the Spanish
viceroy in Lima, who in turn referred to Madrid the question of what to do
about Teixeira. The answer: have him return to Pará, but in the company of
a Spanish representative who would take careful notes en route, then immediately continue to Madrid to share his information. Chosen to lead the Spanish
clerical delegation was Father Cristóbal de Acuña, a Jesuit whose brother was
a powerful military figure in the colonies of western South America. His
presence was insufficient to prevent Teixeira from stopping while en route
downriver at the confluence of the Napo and Aguarico rivers. There he placed
a frontier marker claiming almost the entire Amazon basin in the name of
Philip IV, *King of Portugal*. The actual mark of delineation, a carved log, was
soon washed away. But for more than a century, until Tordesillas was formally
revoked in 1750, Portugal continued to base its tenuous land claim on Teixeira's
acte de présence.

After a voyage of ten months, Acuña landed with Teixeira in Pará in December 1639. He immediately proceeded to Madrid and presented his report
to the court. Before his findings could be widely circulated, however, Portugal
rebelled in 1640 and won freedom from the Spanish crown. For fear that the
priest's intelligence might fall into Portuguese hands, the Spanish court attempted to suppress Acuña's document after its publication in 1641. A few
copies survived, however, and eventually appeared in English translation. The
work is of prime significance, for it is the first in Amazonian history that goes
beyond the narration of sheer survival, and hazards an optimistic assessment
of the region's economic importance. In this regard Acuña foreshadowed the
naturalists and businessmen of the eighteenth and nineteenth centuries who,
likewise, were to reach glowing conclusions about Amazonia's potential.

His work, entitled *A New Discovery of the Great River of the Amazons*, may simply be a recital of his observations, as he—and several other Spanish priests who accompanied the party—jointly recorded them. To some extent the document's bullish findings may have been politically motivated as well, although the author swears to the accuracy of the account. In any event, during their voyage Acuña and his colleagues took great care to note, measure, assess, and evaluate everything they encountered. Having offered suggestions about the great size of the river, they provide details about the bountiful supplies of food and drink that were then available to Amazonian Indians, and the great skills they displayed in acquiring and using them. Their ways of preparing manioc root and palm products are surveyed. Acuña reviews the many attributes of the Amazonian "*pegebuey,*" his term for the *peixe-boi,* or manatee, an eight-foot aquatic mammal that now is all but extinct. "This fish supports itself solely on the herbage on which it browses, as if it were in reality a bullock," Acuña exults. "And from this circumstance the flesh derives so good a flavor, and is so nutritious, that a small quantity leaves a person better satisfied and more vigorous than if he had eaten double the amount of mutton." Turtle likewise tastes "like tender beef," and its fat is "the best and most delicate grease of all." Since "one turtle suffices to satisfy the largest family," Acuña concludes that "these barbarians never know what hunger is."

As further evidence of their food resources, Acuña notes the abundance of fish in the rivers and the sophistication of the Indians' (usually bow-and-arrow) fishing techniques. When they "tire of eating fish alone," the Indians can also turn to the ample supplies of small mammals and game birds that are to be found within the forest. The Indians themselves were friendly and generous. They "made provisions for our lodging, which took some time," Acuña reported, and they willingly shared their own food with the travelers. Moreover, wrote Acuña, "This did not happen on any particular day, but during the whole time the voyage lasted."

In his description of life there, Acuña also inadvertently became the first Amazonian visitor to make careful observations of the uses to which the indigenous peoples put native plants. The good father's ethnobotanical survey includes particular mention of the honey produced by wild bees; of the oil from the *advirova,* with "priceless value for curing wounds"; of the "balsam" from the *copaíba;* and of so many other "herbs and trees of very peculiar qualities" that "a second Dioscorides or a third Pliny should come out, to investigate their properties." Twentieth-century science is, in fact, confirming his observation that "in the wild forests, the natives have, for their sicknesses, the best dispensary of medicines." Such are the forest's timber resources that "in this river vessels may be built better and at less cost than in any other country, finished and launched, without the necessity of sending anything from Europe, except iron for the nails." Not only timber, but cocoa, tobacco, sugar, cotton, and sarsaparilla are other great resources. Since the river "receives affluents from all the richest lands of America," the basin must surely contain undiscovered reserves of precious metals "richer than all the mines of Peru."

According to Acuña, the Indians inhabiting this wonderland were as clever as they were resourceful. They made tools and weapons from turtle shell and manatee skin. Though "most of them go about naked," they usually possessed cotton and knew how to use it. If some seemed more "advanced" than others (the Omáguas were wearing woven clothes), Acuña generally found the Amazonian Indians to "have clear understandings, and rare abilities for any manual dexterity. They are meek and gentle. They gave us their houses to live in . . . and though they suffered much mischief from our friendly Indians, without the possibility of avoiding it, they never returned it by evil acts. All this, together with the slight inclination they display to worship their own gods, gives great hope that, if they received notice of the true Creator of heaven and earth, they would embrace His holy law with little hesitation." Were it not for the "plague of mosquitoes which abound in many places," in fact, Acuña could see little reason why Amazonia should not be "proclaimed with open mouth to be one vast paradise."

Not even Acuña's description of this neo-Arcadia prompted many Spaniards, beyond the occasional missionary, to descend into Amazonia from the "eyebrow" of the Andes. There was gold and silver aplenty in the mountains themselves, and an ample supply of local manpower. In contrast, the Portuguese moved to consolidate their still-tenuous toeholds at Belém and São Luís by spreading inland. Whereas the Northern European traders had maintained friendly relations with the Indians, the Portuguese notion of conquest—political and religious—soon led to conflict. Slavery replaced cooperation as the nature of the relationship between natives and colonists. Missionaries, soldiers, and civilian settlers were soon competing to secure this form of manpower. Jesuits achieved effective control for most of the latter part of the seventeenth century. In mission villages scattered about the lower Amazon, they strove to "reduce" Indians to Christianity, at the same time founding a slave-based economic system that, for the most part, functioned independently of other civil or military authority. Some Indians, themselves slaves, lived in missions or "*aldeias*" and cooperated with the Portuguese in their efforts to capture others from the interior.

Early experiments at plantation agriculture failed. Once the Portuguese had exhausted the most readily available of the *drogas do sertão*—the plant resources of the forest, such as cocoa and what was known as "wild clove"—poverty soon became widespread in the lower Amazon. Few ships came into the port to trade. Portuguese buildings, constructed not of native materials such as thatch but of earth and brick, proved unable to withstand rain and termites. Smallpox arrived from Pernambuco (Recife) as early as 1621, and succeeding epidemics occurred frequently for the next 140 years. The Indians were particularly susceptible: forty thousand died in 1660 and more than twenty thousand just nine years later. Survivors deserted the mission villages and dispersed into the safety of the forests. Conditions became taxing even for the healthy. The historian David Graham Sweet described the conditions: "Food, which had been extraordinarily abundant during the first years of the colony, became chronically scarce with the depletion of soils, the decline of agriculture and the over-hunting and over-fishing of areas immediately adjacent to the towns. In Belém, there was not so much as a slaughterhouse or a store selling the everyday food staples of Portuguese households until well into the eighteenth century."

In *Red Gold*, his exhaustive account of the conquest of Brazil's Indians, the British historian John Hemming thus summarized the state of the region at mid-seventeenth century:

> The Amazon has been depicted as a place of legendary wealth and potential. People forgot all the failures of attempts to colonize it during the past century, and believed the propaganda. It was in reality a tawdry backwater in European terms, with less than a thousand white settlers in both Maranhão and Pará. The towns were clusters of thatched huts, with streets known only by the name of someone who lived on them, or some feature like the local gallows. Sugar did not grow well there, and the only lucrative crops were tobacco, cotton, and a few dyes and medicinal plants gathered from the forests. Movement was entirely by river as the forests were too dense or flooded for roads. The pioneers' farms were clearings on the river banks, and their labour was local Indians—for they were too poor to afford African slaves. There was no minted money until the eighteenth century: the only currency was cotton cloth or barter in other commodities, including Indian slaves. It is awesome to contemplate the destruction caused by those few settlers. The banks of the main stream of the mighty Amazon were almost depopulated and Indians were stripped from the accessible stretches of its tributaries. The populous villages seen by Orellana and Acuña were gone, overgrown by jungle, with their tribes fled or annihilated by the white men's diseases and extortions.

A few isolated voices were raised in favor of better treatment for the Indians and more attention from Lisbon to the needs of the precarious colony. In the western Amazon, itinerant Spanish Jesuits did what they could to curb Portuguese encroachment and devastation. None of these was braver or hardier than a Bohemian named Samuel Fritz, who, in 1686, was sent from Quito to the Marañón to found a mission among the Omáguas. For thirty-seven years the indefatigable Father Fritz traveled the river from its sources to Pará, becoming the first to chart its entire course. During his voyages, often solo, he won the deep confidence of the Indians as he sought to protect them from the slave traders and to improve the degraded quality of their lives. Soon he became enough of a nuisance to the Portuguese that in 1690 they arrested him and kept him imprisoned in Pará for almost two years. Fighting illness and inattention to the plight of his charges, Fritz continued to work among them until 1713. From Portugal a prominent Jesuit named Father Antônio Vieira, who had become an influential adviser to King João IV, was so dismayed to learn of the Indians' plight that he left the court and, in 1653, returned to Amazonia where he had previously worked as a young missionary. Soon after his second arrival, he wrote passionately to the king to complain of exploitation and call for social justice for the beleaguered Indians; later he even returned to Lisbon to press his case. The settlers ended up winning over the Jesuits after many years of intrigue, however, and Vieira passed his later years in frustrated eclipse. On the Spanish side, meanwhile, few were willing to join with Fritz in his effort to oppose Portugal's continuing occupation and consolidation of the basin. The seventeenth century thus became the critical moment when Portuguese hegemony over the region began to be asserted, and

Father Antônio Vieira

when—for want of effective opposition—the mentality of extractivism came
to prevail in Amazonia.

In the late seventeenth and early eighteenth centuries, Portugal continued
to dominate Amazonia with equally little effort. One reason was that, despite
the consistent Portuguese overstepping of the Tordesillas line, Spain was in a
poor position to oppose it. The Hapsburg court that ruled in Madrid until
1700 was indolent and corrupt. The Bourbons who then came to power were
preoccupied with the continuing struggle against Great Britain that had erupted
periodically ever since the debacle of the Spanish Armada in 1588, and was
currently taking such forms as the colorfully named War of Jenkins' Ear. So
busy was Spain elsewhere, in fact, that in 1750 King Ferdinand VI even agreed
to the suggestion of the dying King João V of Portugal that the Tordesillas
issue be resolved by means of a new Treaty of Madrid. Applying the doctrine
of *uti possidetis*, which was to become a critical factor in land-tenure cases more
than two hundred years later, Spain formally ceded to Portugal squatters' rights
to all of the Amazonian territory that it had long effectively controlled. Thus
was peace between Spain and Portugal finally achieved after more than a
century of conflict, and thus ended the era of tension in Amazonia that had
begun with Teixeira's unexpected arrival in Quito 112 years before.

Soon after the signing of the epochal Treaty of Madrid, the forceful Marquês
de Pombal, then in full charge of the Portuguese empire's foreign affairs, sought
to capitalize on the territorial gains by means of new policies whose objective
was to promote colonization and development of the lands of which Portugal
was now legally in possession. Because they interfered with the "free enterprise"
of the slave trade, now almost entirely in African blacks for coastal sugar
plantations, he expelled the Jesuits from Brazil and from Amazonia. Ironically,
expecting that an energetic burst of activity would result, he also decreed
freedom for Amazonia's already decimated and disease-ridden Indians. The
hoped-for boom in Amazonia failed to materialize, however, and the region's
economy worsened, if anything, until the advent of the rubber era a hundred
years later. Meanwhile, few followed the example of pioneers such as Acuña
and Fritz by searching for Amazonian values other than slaves, gold, or other
products of immediate economic value. It remained for new generations of
European visitors to view Amazonia neither from the standpoint of survival,
as had the first arrivals, nor with the hope of quickly achieving power or
economic gain, but with an eye to harvesting its rich if delicate biological
resources.

A natty young Frenchman named Charles-Marie de La Condamine is often
credited with inaugurating the new era of scientific research and discovery in
Amazonia. An aristocrat, born into the court of Louis XIV in 1701, La Condamine became a brilliant mathematician and won his admittance to the Académie des Sciences at the age of only twenty-nine. His special interest was the

The Marquês de Pombal

Charles-Marie de La Condamine

size and shape of the earth, statistics that were still imperfectly understood by geographers of the era. One important calculation in dispute was the length of one arc of the meridian, or one degree of latitude. To take measurements that would help to establish a precise figure (a British source already had it right, at sixty nautical miles per degree, or one mile per minute of latitude), the Académie in 1735 planned two expeditions: one to Lapland and the other to the Equator. With the help of his good friend Voltaire, La Condamine won a leading role on the equatorial trip, which had been commissioned by King Louis XV and had been promised assistance in America by his fellow Bourbon, King Philip of Spain. With ten scientific colleagues and a considerable entourage, La Condamine arrived in Quito in 1736. The group remained in the province, engaged in scientific work that suffered interminable delays, for seven years. During the course of the visit the fearless and energetic La Condamine heard much about the Amazon and determined to return to Europe via the river and Pará. For this voyage, rather than for the previous years he had tediously spent measuring the planet, he finally became best known.

La Condamine completed the trip over a four-month period late in 1744 in the company of Don Pedro Maldonado, a Spanish explorer and naturalist who was then governor of the Peruvian province of Esmeraldas. Leaving Quito, the party proceeded by foot, horse, and canoe down into Amazonia from the Andes. At Borja, on the upper Amazon, La Condamine looked out over the dense green forests and wrote: "I found myself in a new world, separated from all human intercourse, on a freshwater sea surrounded by a maze of lakes, rivers, and canals and penetrating in every direction the gloom of an immense forest. New plants, new animals, and new races of man were exhibited to my view. Accustomed during seven years to mountains lost in clouds, I was rapt with admiration at the wide circle embraced by the eye, restricted here by no other boundary than the horizon."

What they accomplished, during the course of a smooth run from Borja to Pará, was the first truly scientific examination of the basin. They observed the use of many medicinal plants, including quinine. They wondered at the properties of rubber—a substance they referred to as "the rosin called *cahout-chou*." "What renders it most remarkable is its great elasticity," La Condamine said of it in his journal. "They [the Indians] make bottles thereof which it is not easy to break; boots, and hollow bowls which may be squeez'd flat, and when no longer under restraint recover their first form." The party observed and admired the properties of curare and other poisons of the forest and saw evidence of the effects of vaccination as a smallpox preventive. But if they joined Acuña in their admiration of the forest's resources and the uses made of them by Indians (whom La Condamine called "Americans") and habituated colonists, La Condamine and Maldonado made an even more basic contribution to Amazonian understanding: a major improvement in geographical knowledge of the basin. They made detailed measurements of the river's rise and fall, the speed of its current, its depth. Using Father Fritz's maps as a basic resource, they made charts whose accuracy has been exceeded only by modern technology—as in the instance of a tributary five hundred miles long that was discovered only with the advent of the satellite remote-sensing technology of the 1970s. Without providing an answer, La Condamine also posed again the question first raised by the voyage of the infamous Lope de Aguirre: the whereabouts of the link between the Amazon and Orinoco river systems. Though he could not provide a precise location, and though savants of the age suppressed the idea and treated it as "chimerical," his conversations with Indians and missionaries left him with no doubt of an "existing communication between the waters of the two rivers."

After his return to Europe in 1745, La Condamine spent his remaining years in a continuing series of debates about the results of his trip. The rubber he brought with him provoked European speculation about the virtues of the substance, and his theories about tropical diseases and remedies proved to be controversial. What he felt about weights and measures was influential in moving Europe toward unity around the metric system. About his theories of Amazonian geography, however, silence prevailed for the remainder of the century. The link between the river systems was a matter not much discussed even by the diligent Alexandre Rodrigues Ferreira, a Brazil-born naturalist who penetrated deep into the Rio Negro during the course of an exhaustive nine-year (1793–92) expedition commissioned by the court in Lisbon. Accompanied by a botanist and two artists, Rodrigues Ferreira made extensive ethnographic and biological collections and successfully shipped them across the Atlantic; the expedition's voluminous sets of watercolors and drawings provided Europe with its first visual evidence ever of many aspects of Amazonian life. But neither Rodrigues Ferreira nor a number of other Portuguese explorers of the late eighteenth century, although motivated by the new sense of activism about Amazonian penetration that had been launched by Pombal, had anything particular to say about the basic geography of the region. Perhaps it was lingering fear of Spain that kept them mute. In any event it was no Portuguese adventurer, but another far-ranging European, the Prussian Baron Alexander von Humboldt, who picked up where La Condamine had left off.

Born near Berlin at the small family castle called Tegel, Humboldt studied political and natural science. He was heavily influenced by Goethe's ideas, distilled from a heady brew containing elements of everything from poetry to botany, and reached an early decision that travels in the neotropics would help him develop no less than a "philosophy of the earth." Accompanied by a faithful colleague, the French botanist Aimé Bonpland, whose sad fate was to die penniless of syphilis in southern Brazil, Humboldt spent the years 1799–1804

in the Americas. Landing in Venezuela, he and Bonpland made their way up
the Orinoco and eventually found the Cassiquiare River or "Canal," thus
becoming the first Europeans to establish and record the connection between
the Orinoco and Amazon river systems at a point, he wrote, where the link
was "arbitrarily suppressed" in the maps they carried. Passing through into
the upper Rio Negro, the Humboldt party visited several Spanish missions,

Baron Alexander von Humboldt camped beside the Orinoco River. *(The Bettmann Archive)*

then planned to venture to the village of Barcelos on the Portuguese side and continue from there to Pará. "We were informed in San Carlos," Humboldt later wrote, "that, on account of political circumstances, it was difficult at that moment to pass from the Spanish to the Portuguese settlements; but we did not know until after our return to Europe the extent of the danger to which we should have been exposed in proceeding as far as Barcelos. It was known in Brazil, perhaps by means of the newspapers, the well-meant but indiscreet zeal of which has so often proved injurious to travelers, that I was going to visit the missions of the Rio Negro, and examine the natural canal, which unites two great systems of rivers. In those desert forests instruments had been seen only in the hands of the commissioners of boundaries; and at that time the subaltern agents of the Portuguese government could [not] conceive... how a man of good sense could expose himself to the fatigues of a long journey 'to measure lands that did not belong to him.' Orders had been issued, to seize my person, my instruments, and above all those registers of astronomical observations, so dangerous to the safety of states. We were to be conducted by way of the Amazon to Grand Pará, and thence sent back to Lisbon."

Humboldt and Bonpland, then, became early victims of the Brazilian paranoia about foreign activity in Amazonia which would often recur. Avoiding capture by continuing westward, the party visited Colombia, Ecuador, and Panama, then Mexico, where they remained for almost a year. They paused in Havana for two months to assemble their collections. Finally, before returning to Europe, Humboldt went to Philadelphia where he made contact with President Jefferson, with whom as a result he spent three weeks in Monticello and Washington before returning to Europe. Later Humboldt consumed his entire fortune in arranging for the publication of thirty-three volumes of his American journals, which, according to one source, became no less than "the basis of all future scientific research on the tropical countries of Latin America." About the upper Rio Negro he achieved an Everest of enthusiasm. "Bonpland assures me that he will lose his mind if the wonders don't cease soon," wrote Humboldt in a letter to his brother. "But more beautiful than these marvels by themselves is the impression made by this vigorous, luxuriant, and yet at the same time so light, exhilarating, and mild plant world as a whole. I feel I shall be very happy here." In some respects his prescriptions for the region's improvement were far from the mark. The productivity of the upper Rio Negro, he felt, would be enhanced not only by the removal of the abundant insects but also "when the destruction of the forests has diminished the excessive humidity of the air and the soil." If Humboldt fell short of becoming the first to foresee a "world breadbasket" role for Amazonia, a great development scheme for the region was surely a centerpiece of the "philosophy" he contrived upon his return to Europe. And his description of the Cassiquiare was revolutionary to European thinkers accustomed to river systems separated by far more clearly defined watersheds.

By the time of Humboldt's travels at the end of the eighteenth century, then, a clear distinction between what visitors thought about Amazonia and what actually went on there had already been established. On the one hand, the paeans of Amazonian beauty and promise, first fully articulated by Father Acuña, were reiterated by such elegant observers as La Condamine and Humbolt himself. But if these statements had aroused curiosity and greed in many corners of Europe, the few Europeans who actually settled in Amazonia had hardly become successful. Thanks to their practices, in fact, conditions in Amazonia had sharply retrogressed since Orellana's epic voyage. Untold numbers of Indians had been enslaved or murdered, or had simply died from exposure to imported diseases to which they had no means of achieving immunity. The colonists' arrival and the introduction of new agricultural methods had caused food to become, if anything, far less plentiful than it had been in the sixteenth century. Sustainable uses for the forest, or for the resources from within the rivers, had yet to be found.

The hapless Madame Godin

There is no more valiant a symbol of the hardship of colonial Amazonia than Madame Godin, the determined wife of a member of La Condamine's party who was compelled to leave her and their two children in Quito. For fifteen years the lady awaited news of a "sloop" that her husband, before continuing into Amazonia, had promised would come to fetch her. Upon hearing a report of a rescue party on the upper Marañón, she decided to try to expedite the rendezvous by setting forth across the Andes with the children, her brother, and several servants. To her dismay, she found the village for which she was headed to have been totally eradicated by smallpox. She therefore was compelled to continue down the Marañón without guides or maps or food. Next she lost her canoe in rapids, and the party continued on foot. Everybody but she died of hunger and fatigue; after nine days of struggling forward alone, she was found by Indians and taken to a mission village. Eventually, after a separation that lasted fully nineteen years, the bedraggled lady was reunited with her husband in Belém.

Such were the realities of life in eighteenth-century Amazonia. Yet the visionary planners—from Portuguese Jesuit bureaucrats who ordered the "reductions" of the Indians, to the Marquês de Pombal and his early plans to exploit Amazonia's resources—still chose to defy them and dream on. In this regard the colonial history of Amazonia accurately heralded the great age of scientific exploration in Amazonia, with its unprecedented flow of exuberant forecasts, the precipitous rubber boom of the late nineteenth century, and then its equally sudden collapse just before World War I.

CHAPTER 4

From Naturalist to Extractivist

THE NINETEENTH-CENTURY TRAVELERS WHO VISITED AMAZONIA WERE very different from the elegant noblemen who had preceded them. Many European scientists were now being deeply influenced by the writings and teachings of the Swedish botanist Linnaeus (Karl von Linné), a forefather of modern botany and taxonomy—the ordering of living things into families and genera and species. While they were being motivated by him to roam widely in order to gather and codify the plants of the tropics, the end of the Napoleonic wars meant that royal minds could wander too. Enthused by what La Condamine and Humboldt had reported, the courts of Europe became eager to mount official expeditions to the tropics, and particularly to Amazonia. There was no lack of qualified scientists and naturalists wanting to participate in them; other professionals found they could support themselves by selling their collections of plants, seeds, skins, and skulls to museums and botanical gardens.

King Max Joseph I of Bavaria, with the assistance of the Austrian court, was the first European crowned head to organize an Amazonian scientific venture. An ardent student of botany, Max Joseph frequented the gardens at Erlangen, often in the company of a young botanist named Karl Friedrich

Karl Friedrich Philipp von Martius   Johann Baptist von Spix

Philipp von Martius, and had long itched to send his own expedition to South America in the footsteps of Humboldt. When Max Joseph heard that the Austrian Archduchess Leopoldina would sail to Brazil as the bride of the crown prince (later Emperor Dom Pedro I), he requested and was granted permission to send Martius as well as a zoologist, Johann Baptist von Spix, across on the same vessel. The young men (Martius was only twenty-three) arrived in Rio de Janeiro in 1817. After extensive studies there, they continued to Belém for a year of research in Amazonia that included travels to the upper Solimões as far as Tabatinga, the Japurá, and the upper Rio Negro.

In their brief visit, the first to Amazonia by European scientists since La Condamine, Spix and Martius amassed the largest collection of Amazonian flora and fauna that anyone had ever achieved. Though Spix died in 1826 and was not able to complete his research and publications on Brazilian animal life, he survived long enough to join Martius in writing the first volume of what was to become a long series. Entitled *Travels in Brazil, 1817–1820*, it was published in 1823. The second and third volumes, written by Martius almost entirely alone (he had some help on fish classifications from the young Swiss professor Louis Agassiz, who was later to mount his own expedition), appeared in 1828 and 1831. Taken as a whole, this major work includes ample material about the natural history of Brazil, its people, and its economic and social conditions; Goethe reportedly praised its "superior style." In addition,

Martius produced his formidable *Flora Brasiliensis*, which contains no fewer than 1,100 illustrations and remains essential reading for contemporary botanists. It was only one of 160 publications on Brazil that the prolific Martius completed up to his death in 1868.

Although the first Spix/Martius volume relates to their travels in southern Brazil, Volumes II and III provide details of their voyages on the upper Solimões and the upper Rio Negro respectively. Martius was a great authority on palm trees and described numerous species for the first time. They didn't get everything right, and where they went wrong is in itself revealing. One example is this passage from Volume I, which, in its description of the environs of Rio de Janeiro (then dense tropical forest), hints at what was later documented about the fragility of the tropical forest, but concludes that the only remedy required is a little good solid European organization:

> With such a fullness of life and such a vigorous striving at development, even so rich and fertile a soil as this is not capable of furnishing the necessary nourishment in sufficient abundance; hence these gigantic trees are in a constant struggle for their own preservation, and impede one another's growth still more than the trees in our forest. Even the stems which have grown to a considerable height, and require a large sample of nutriment, feel the influence of their more powerful neighbors, are suddenly arrested in their growth by being deprived of the requisite juices, and thus become in a short time subject to the general powers of nature, which lead them to rapid dissolution.... When at some future period a regular system of forest cultivation ... shall be introduced, it will be found necessary not so much to promote the growth of the trees close together as to take care that they stand at a sufficient distance from each other.

In a subsequent passage, the two Bavarians foresee a future era in Brazil when "the inhabitants have cut down the woods, drained marshes, made roads, everywhere founded villages and towns, and thus by degrees triumphed over the rank vegetation ... all the elements will willingly ... recompense the activity of man. But before Brazil has attained this period of civilization, the uncultivated land may yet prove a grave to thousands of adventurers." If Spix and Martius had a keen eye for what the intense competition for light and nutrients meant within the forest, their prescription for its improvement by means of its clear-cutting was a well-meaning but uninformed precursor of the disastrous development policies that would be advanced by Brazil's government fully 150 years later.

At midcentury, after many lesser government-sponsored expeditions had come and gone, there arrived in Amazonia that remarkable trio of English naturalists who helped prompt my visit to the Uaupés: Alfred Russel Wallace,

Alfred Russel Wallace

Richard Spruce

Henry Walter Bates

who, with Darwin, helped to develop the theory of natural selection; the entomologist Henry Walter Bates; and Richard Spruce, a botanist of prime importance in the evolution of thought about Amazonia. A schoolteacher in the town of Leicester, the young Wallace had been greatly impressed by Darwin's *Voyage of the Beagle* and had become determined to embark on his own excursion to the neotropics. In Bates, at the time apprentice to a hosiery manufacturer and a passionate bug collector in his spare time, Wallace found a kindred spirit. Determined to mount an expedition "towards solving the problem of the origin of species," as Wallace phrased it in a letter to Bates, the two young men (Wallace was twenty-five, Bates twenty-three) sought and won commissions to send collections back to England. They set forth in 1848 and landed in Belém, which with a population of fifteen thousand was the largest settlement anywhere in Amazonia. After several months of increasingly productive viewing and collecting there, they proceeded upstream to Santarém and later to Manaus. Here they split. Choosing the Rio Negro, Wallace probed the Uaupés, recovered from the fever that felled him at São Joaquim, then hastened downriver to Belém. He was back in England by 1853 after a five-year stay. Bates chose the upper Solimões as his principal research area, and there spent most of his total of eleven years in Amazonia. Both wrote what became classic journals of their travels as well as numerous scientific papers.

Malaria was far from the only major problem that Wallace encountered during his Amazonian travels. While he was en route home to England, his ship caught fire and he spent ten days drifting aboard an open lifeboat, losing most of his collection, before being rescued by a passing vessel. He was to achieve his greatest fame for the accounts of his later adventures among the islands and peoples of the Malayan archipelago. His regard for the Indians of Amazonia was limited—he called them animals—even though he admired some of their practices. As for the mixed population of Amazonia's cities, he displayed a sense of outrage. "Morals in Barra (later Manaus) are perhaps at the lowest ebb possible in any civilised community," he sniffed in his *Travels on the Amazon and Rio Negro.* "You will every day hear things commonly talked of, about the most respectable families in the place, which would hardly be credited of the inhabitants of the worst parts of St. Giles's." Despite the severity of Wallace's troubles, and the disdain he expressed for the humans in Amazonia, no other naturalist in the region displayed a greater sense of passion about the challenge of scientific discovery there, or more fervent optimism about the region's potential. Here, for instance, is how Wallace described his reactions to his discovery of a new insect species:

The beauty and brilliance of this insect are indescribable, and none but a naturalist can understand the intense excitement I experienced when I at last captured it. On taking it out of my net and opening the glorious wings, my heart began to beat violently, the blood rushed to my head, and I felt more like fainting than I have done when in apprehension of immediate death. I had a headache the rest of the day, so great was the excitement produced by what will appear to most people a very inadequate cause.

And if Wallace had little good to say about the people of Amazonia, he could hardly say enough about the potential of the region itself:

It is a vulgar error, copied and repeated from one book to another, that in the tropics the luxuriance of the vegetation overpowers the efforts of man. Just the reverse is the case: nature and climate are nowhere so favourable to the laborer and I fearlessly assert that here, the 'primeval' forest can be converted into rich pasture and meadow land, into cultivated fields, gardens and orchards, containing every variety of produce, with half the labour and, what is of more importance, in less than half the time that would be required at home, even though there we had clear, instead of forest ground to commence upon.

For his part, Bates had as bad a time as any visitor in Amazonia since Madame Godin. He was bitten by ticks, mosquitoes, ants, and countless other kinds of insects. Bats sucked his blood and he faced threats from jaguars, alligators, piranhas, and snakes. He suffered from food "privations" and illnesses, including malaria. He was robbed and left penniless by an Indian employee, and at one stage in his travels, having not received a remittance from London for more than a year, he was reduced to going shoeless and wearing rags. His attitude toward the Amazonian "red man," in whom he detected "fundamental defects of character" and an "almost total absence of curiosity," was hardly more charitable than Wallace's. Bates was even the first student of Amazonia to come away with the impression that its then small population was already draining the basin of certain resources. He reported a great reduction in the turtle-egg harvest in one region, adding that according to the Indians "formerly the waters teemed as thickly with turtles as the air now does with mosquitoes."

Yet no other field naturalist was more successful in Amazonia than was Bates. He collected more than fourteen thousand species of insects and animals, and eight thousand of them were brand new to science. He safely shipped almost everything to London; his collections were studied by scientists the world over, and are treasured even today. He was remarkably cheerful in adversity and could put a good face upon almost anything. After one particularly grueling voyage he wrote. "Notwithstanding the hard fare, the confinement of the canoe, the trying weather, frequent and drenching rains, with gleams of fiery sunshine, and the woeful desolation of the river scenery, I enjoyed the voyage as a whole." He called the region's climate "the most enjoyable on the face of the earth," and was a quintessential booster of its overall prospects. "The imagination becomes excited," he wrote, "when one reflects upon the possible future of this place, situated near the centre of the equatorial part of South America, in the midst of a region almost as large as Europe, every inch of whose soil is of the most exuberant fertility, and having water communication on one side with the Atlantic, and on the other with the Spanish republics."

The Amazon became the core of his life. After his eleven years on the river, he returned to London to write his classic *The Naturalist on the River Amazons*. In 1864 he became Assistant Secretary of the Royal Geographic Society. One can easily imagine the little bug collector from Leeds aging gracefully and telling Amazonian tales to any Londoner willing to listen.

Like Wallace, Spruce as a young man was smitten by Darwin's findings and speculations. He became determined to do for botany in the tropics what Darwin had done elsewhere in the natural sciences. A self-trained botanist who earned his living as a schoolteacher in Yorkshire, he had little money and suffered from ill health. Overall, Spruce seems a poor prospect to have become one of the towering figures of Amazonian science. Determination prevailed, however. His articles in *The Phytologist*, a journal that began publication in 1841, brought him to the attention of curators at Kew Gardens. Through one of them, Sir Willian Hooker, Spruce met a botanical collector named George Bentham, who persuaded him that the expenses of a tropical voyage could easily be covered through sales of dried plants, well preserved and accurately identified, to herbariums and museums. After Spruce had completed a trial two-year collecting trip to Spain, Bentham advanced him the funds for an Amazonian venture and agreed to act as his agent in Britain. Spruce set sail for Brazil in 1849, at the age of thirty-two, and caught up with Bates and Wallace in Santarém a year later.

Thus began another of the most comprehensive scientific examinations of Amazonia ever undertaken by a lone individual. Of his total of fifteen years there, Spruce spent the first six (until 1864) wandering up the Rio Negro to São Gabriel and then the Orinoco. It was during this time that he ventured into the Uaupés and nursed the malaria-stricken Wallace. During his remaining nine years he explored the Solimões westward to the foothills of the Andes. He collected meticulously and was careful to describe in great detail everything that he found and shipped off to Kew. Yet his giant contribution to Amazonian plant taxonomy, still so well recognized that his lovingly preserved collections at Kew remain a Mecca for the world's tropical botanists, represents only a small portion of his overall accomplishment. He saw Amazonia not merely as a series of trees and plants, each to be identified and assigned to a genus or species, but as a complex ecosystem in which the smallest parts bore some sort of relationship to the whole. With unprecedented precision he described the characteristics of the forest, from the dimensions of its greatest trees to the shapes of the petals on the smallest flowers. He wrote of lianas or "rope plants" with one-foot diameters which spiraled up the tree trunks; of seed dispersal mechanisms and other examples of plant-animal relations in the forest; of the large grass islands that sweep down the rivers during the flood seasons, often carrying large mammals aboard; of the region's geology as best he could decipher it; of beetles and butterflies and fish. He amassed a formidable collection of thirty thousand plants, and discovered and described no less than seven thousand species that were new to European science. He studied the Indians' usage of wild plant materials, often himself sampling those said to have medicinal properties. His comments and papers on the subject greatly advanced the level of ethnobotanical knowledge of Amazonia.

So keen a student of Amazonia was Spruce that it would not have been surprising if he had begun to sniff out the evidence of its vulnerability. He did, at least, come forward with evidence of the great variety within Amazonia, and of the paucity of life in some of its corners, referring to the Rio Negro as a "dead river." Even near Belém, he observed that "in some places one might walk for a considerable distance without seeing a single herb, or even rarely a fallen leaf, on the bare black ground." Certainly his own thorough

Stilt roots, or what Spruce called *sapopemas* (*Doug Shane*)

work provoked great admiration throughout Europe. In 1864, for instance, the German Academy awarded him an honorary degree. He represented part of a scientific continuum that led to the publication in 1898 of *Plant Geography*, the great work by the German botanist A. F. W. Schimper, and the subsequent beginnings of soil science and ecology in Germany and in Britain early in the twentieth century. He encountered the usual difficulties with insects, storms, hunger, capsizing canoes, and malaria.

Yet Spruce's own analyses of the forest's phenomena usually reached upbeat endings, and once again revealed little firm knowledge of the frailty of the forests he was studying with such great intensity. He noted, for example, that Amazonian trees typically lack taproots thrusting directly downward, but instead are buttressed by *sapopemas* or crowns of outward-spreading roots at the bottom of their trunks. The reason for this adaptation, as scientists of the twentieth century have established, has to do with the lack of topsoil in Amazonia and the highly competitive search for scarce nutrients in which plants there must engage if their species are to survive. To Spruce, though, it seemed most likely that "a rocky matrix, bare or thinly covered with earth, may have been the main origin of *sapopemas*, for it is in such sites that the most numerous and perfect examples of them exist at this day."

Overall, Spruce joined Bates and Wallace in expressing passionate confidence about the basin's future. He even came to agree with Sir Walter Raleigh, who had almost persuaded Queen Elizabeth I that England should destroy and replace the Spanish American empire, but later fell into disfavor with her successor, King James I, for having failed to find gold in Guiana. "How often," wrote Spruce, "have I regretted that England did not possess the magnificent Amazon Valley instead of India! If that booby James, instead of putting Raleigh in prison and finally cutting off his head, had persevered in supplying him with ships, money and men until he had formed a permanent establishment on one of the great American rivers, I have no doubt but that the whole American continent would have been at this moment in the hands of the English race!"

Though Queen Victoria failed to respond to Spruce's exhortation, Amazonia remained to the end the center of his own life. In 1864, having seen remarkable change in Amazonia as the rubber era took off, he returned to England. For seventeen further years, plagued by intermittent illness, he pushed forward at the Herculean task of organizing his Amazonian notes and papers, and was still at it when he died in 1893. Wallace then took up Spruce's unfinished work. After extensive editing and condensing, he arranged for the publication, in 1908, of the Spruce volume *Notes of a Botanist on the Amazon, 1849–1864*. Though little noticed when it first appeared, this narrative equals the accounts of Wallace and Bates as the third classic nineteenth-century tale of Amazonia.

In 1846 an explorer and naturalist named W. H. Edwards, the first American to travel in Amazonia and write extensively about his experiences there, ascended the river from Belém to Manaus and made a number of side trips into the forest to explore and to collect specimens. He described his experiences in 1847, in a volume entitled *A Voyage up the River Amazon*. Containing the usual optimistic forecasts of Amazonia's future, this work appeared at a moment when the Monroe Doctrine and the concept of Manifest Destiny both served as justification for U.S. reaction to European initiatives in the Western Hemisphere. Yet the principal response to Edwards's narrative was in Britain, where both Bates and Wallace read and admired it. During the 1850s the very first "official" U.S. expedition to the region was mounted, with Naval Lieutenants Herndon and Gibbon at the helm. Their mission, far from hegemonic, was to see if the United States could use the region to rid itself of the embarrassment of slavery. The report of their canoe trip down the river, undertaken in 1851 and completed the following year, provided little information about the prospects for a mass transmigration of Southern plantation owners and their entourages, nor did it provide encouragement about the basin's agricultural potential. Nevertheless, it aroused sufficient interest to help bring on a flurry of southward-bound expeditions over the following decades.

Professor Louis Agassiz *(The Bettmann Archive)*

The Thayer expedition, named in honor of the Bostonian financier who paid for it, was the first of these. It was mounted in 1865 by Harvard's resplendent zoologist Louis Agassiz, who arrived with a towering reputation built in his native Switzerland, but became controversial in the United States because of his opposition to Darwin's theories. Such was his prestige, though, that Agassiz had little difficulty in arranging to visit Amazonia, principally in order to continue the studies of the region's fishes that he had begun under Martius, and to assemble a collection of materials for a new zoology museum at the university. U.S. government contacts assured the Agassiz party, which numbered six scientists and a substantial supporting cast, of a quasi-royal reception in Brazil from the moment of their landing in Rio de Janeiro to their departure from the northern coast two years later. The narrative of their wanderings and discoveries, which included a questionable analysis of the basin's geological history, was assembled and published in breathless detail by the professor's second wife, Elizabeth Cary Agassiz, who was later to become a founder of Radcliffe College and its first president. She found much to criticize about Amazonia: indolence, lack of proper sanitation, a "melancholy" air, and a "general aspect of incompleteness and decay." As she put it in the expedition's journal: "In the midst of a country which should be overflowing with agricultural products, neither milk, nor butter, nor cheese, nor vegetables, nor fruit, are to be had.... You constantly hear people complaining of the difficulty of procuring even the commonest articles of domestic consumption when, in fact, they ought to be produced by every land-owner."

Doubtful that the Brazilians would ever make much of Amazonia, Professor and Mrs. Agassiz envisioned a new era of internationalization "when the banks of the Amazons will teem with a population more active and vigorous than any it has yet seen—when all civilizations will share in its wealth, when the twin continents will shake hands and Americans of the North come to help Americans of the South in developing its resources." Naturally, these resources existed, and the Agassizes' abiding faith is revealed in this curious passage from the journal:

> When I remember the poor people I have seen in the watch-making and lace-making villages of Switzerland, hardly lifting their eyes from the break of day till night, and even then earning barely enough to keep them above actual want, and think how easily everything grows here, on land to be had for almost nothing, it seems a pity that some parts of the world should be so overstocked that there is not nourishment for all, and others so empty that there are none to gather the harvest. We long to see a vigorous emigration pour into this region so favored by Nature, so bare of inhabitants.

(After Brazil's slave era ended in 1888, emigration from Europe did in fact become a central element in Brazilian policy. In 1891, three-quarters of a million

Europeans arrived, mostly from Italy but also from Germany and Austria, to found farms and colonies in the bountiful center and south of the country. Few ended up in Amazonia, glowingly said by Agassiz to have the potential to accommodate no fewer than 300 million inhabitants.)

In the aftermath of the Thayer expedition, other American naturalists and explorers were to follow, to collect for natural history museums or botanical gardens, or simply to explore. In 1912 one of the region's most illustrious visitors, Theodore Roosevelt, undertook a voyage down the basin's southern tributaries and into the lower Amazon via the Madeira. En route, he almost drowned when a canoe capsized in rapids. Roosevelt also suffered from hunger and from a suppurating abscess. Yet not even the tale of his Amazonian adventures attracted great interest in the States. At no time did any great movement of U.S. citizens into Amazonia take place, except for a small influx of fugitive Confederates after the Civil War. Organized by one Major Warren Hastings, this group arrived in Santarém in 1866 and began to work land granted by the imperial government. "A few years later," wrote the Brazilian historian Leandro Tocantins in his recent book *Amazonia—Nature, Man and Time*, "various North American families returned to their own country, disillusioned with the climate, with land that favored neither their agriculture, nor the idealizations of the life style from which they thought they would benefit." For all the centuries of foreign interest and travels, in fact, it was the "indolent" Brazilians themselves who finally led the charge into Amazonia.

Christopher Columbus had returned to the Spanish court with tales and samples of strange bouncing balls that he had been given by Indians in the Caribbean. Various other explorers of South America and the Caribbean had spoken of similar miracles. La Condamine had seen the substance the Indians called *cahout-chou* (the weeping tree). Soon after his arrival in Quito in 1736, he sent seeds and samples to Paris. In 1745, after his return to Europe, he described in detail to the Académie Française the process by which the latex (a word he derived from *leche*, the Spanish word for milk) from the trees was transformed into rubber, and in turn into the pumps and syringes that the Indians made of the substance. During the latter half of the eighteenth century, rubber products fashioned by Amazonian Indians began to trickle into Europe, where they aroused considerable if casual curiosity. By 1800, in spite of trade restrictions imposed by the Portuguese, Belém-manufactured products such as rubber shoes and pencil erasers had appeared in North America as well as in Europe. Exports of Amazonian rubber multiplied as little factories sprang up in those countries.

In the United States the inventor Charles Goodyear, son of an unsuccessful Naugatuck, Connecticut, hardware merchant, had a string of failures to his own credit when, in 1834, he became intrigued by rubber's properties. Soon he realized that its basic problem had to do with temperature. Tackling the

Theodore Roosevelt in Amazonia, in his camp and swimming
(Courtesy of the Library Services Department, American Museum of Natural History)

Exterior and interior views of the Manaus opera house

question with obsessive enthusiasm, in 1844 he invented the process of vulcanization, which prevented rubber products from becoming brittle in cold weather and multiplied the number of uses to which the substance could be put. Exports rose steadily each decade in the latter half of the nineteenth century, and took off in the 1890s after John Boyd Dunlop invented the pneumatic rubber tire. In 1910, rubber represented a remarkable 40 percent of all Brazilian exports. The maximum volume of 44,296 tons exported (versus eight in 1827, 6,590 in 1870, and a 21,000-ton average during the 1890s) was achieved in 1911.

While the fun lasted, life in the principal cities of Amazonia during the *belle époque* reached giddy levels not since approached. I can find no evidence that Enrico Caruso, although widely credited with the accomplishment, ever actually sang in Manaus. But many other stars and companies did perform in its stylish opera house as well as at the less renowned but equally impressive theater in Belém. In just a few decades, Belém and Manaus grew from the scruffy villages that Bates and Wallace visited into handsome towns with broad boulevards and impressive Beaux Arts buildings. Bates had not been greatly moved by the changes. Manaus, he snorted, "was once a pleasant place of residence, but it is now in a most wretched plight, suffering from a chronic scarcity of the most necessary articles of food. Now the neighborhood does not produce even mandioca-meal sufficient for its own consumption. Many of the most necessary articles of food, besides all luxuries, come from Portugal, England and North America."

That was just the way most Europeans in Amazonia wanted it. "*Quelle différence*," wrote one French visitor at the height of the boom, between stately Belém and the disorderly cities of southern Brazil. He added the ultimate compliment: that Belém reminded him of Marseilles or Bordeaux. There were fine restaurants and elegant bordellos supplied with European talent. Some residents of Amazonia were even said to have sent their laundry to Europe. In just a decade, Amazonia's population mushroomed from 300,000 to well over a million.

If not quite so elegantly, Brazil during the nineteenth century had achieved nationhood. Geographical boundaries, according to Brazil extending almost as far west as Teixeira's marker, had been legalized with the signing of the Treaty of Madrid in 1750. Once in firm control of the largest single tract of land on the South American continent, the Portuguese became more keenly interested in retaining it. Politics in Europe played an important role as well. In 1807 Napoleon invaded Portugal. Rather than abandon their alliance with the British by accepting subservience to France, Queen Maria de Braganza and Regent Dom João resolved simply to transfer the entire court to Brazil and, with British naval assistance, managed to do so. After France and Portugal made peace as the Napoleonic fortunes declined, Dom João (now Emperor

João VI, since Maria had died) returned to Europe to reclaim his throne and
left his son Pedro in Rio de Janeiro to act as regent. Relations then worsened
between father and son, with an unexpected and fateful result: in 1822, defying
Dom João's command, Dom Pedro refused to return to Portugal and declared
Brazil to be independent. Almost two decades of court intrigue were to follow
before Brazil steadied on course as a constitutional monarchy. But by 1840
Dom Pedro's son, the scholarly Dom Pedro II, had been installed as emperor
at the age of fourteen. His governance was to last for fully forty-nine years
and was notable for its wisdom and integrity. It reached a progressive if stormy
end when, warned that he would be dethroned if he abolished slavery without
compensation for the owners, Dom Pedro followed his instinct. He was con-
veniently out of the country in 1888 when his daughter, Princess Isabel, decreed
unconditional emancipation. During the ensuing turmoil Dom Pedro, old and
ailing with diabetes, again left Brazil in 1889, after the republic had been
proclaimed and a revolutionary government formed. Brazil thus manifested
an early talent for achieving bloodless if sudden changes in government.

Emperor Dom Pedro II

During the monarchy, Amazonia's allegiances were divided between Europe and southern Brazil. Ties to the south were tightened as Brazilian nationhood took shape and as steamship service, which began in 1852 and for fifteen years remained exclusively national, became increasingly frequent between the basin and the ports of Recife, Rio de Janeiro, and Santos. But to many, the mounting exuberance of the rubber era also foretold a day when Brazil as a whole would achieve the dream of international *grandeza* (greatness) that had proved elusive in the seventeenth century, when she lost her brief dominance of the world sugar market. Pressure (some from Professor Agassiz, who had corresponded frequently with Dom Pedro II even before he toured Brazil) grew to open the Amazon to foreign ships. Internationalism prevailed as Brazilian confidence waxed, and by the 1870s the great vessels of the Booth Line, the Hamburg-Amerika Line, and the Red Cross Line had begun to ply the river. But the rubber boom, instead of catapulting Brazil into long-term prosperity in the world's markets and into great-nation status, ended, as World War I began, with the sudden violence of an afternoon squall in Amazonia.

The denouement had been quietly brewing for several decades. In 1875 a clever British planter named Henry A. Wickham had begun to ship seeds of the native Brazilian rubber tree, *Hevea brasiliensis*, to Sir Joseph Dalton Hooker, son of Spruce's mentor, at Kew Gardens in London, so that they could be forwarded to Asia for cultivation under controlled circumstances. After a few false starts, growers in Asia (principally Malaya) succeeded in establishing plantations based on the Brazilian seedlings. When the trees matured, rubber could be harvested from the tidy Asian plantations, their trees positioned in tight rows, at far less cost than from the wild trees dispersed in the Amazonian forest. From only nine percent of the world's output in 1910, Asian production grew to equal Amazonia's by 1913, and then soared rapidly ahead. Why had Brazil stumbled so badly? For one thing, wrote the prominent scientist Harald Sioli, "Nobody thought of establishing artificial plantations of rubber trees since the general idea was that the world would depend forever on the Amazonian rubber." But if Brazilian shortsightedness was involved, there was a still-unrecognized ecological problem as well: as Henry Ford was soon to discover (see Chapter 5), rubber plantations in Amazonia would not have worked even if they had been established as a way to compete with the Asian producers. The reason is a disease called the South American leaf blight (*Dothidella ulei*) that is bothersome to plant life only in the neotropics and is particularly harmful to rubber trees. As long as they are scattered in the wild Amazonian forest, the trees are not greatly affected by the blight. Once they are planted close together, though, *Dothidella* has proved to be lethal to them.

If ecological factors were involved, the environmental (though not the human) consequences of the boom were in fact limited. Since most of the rubber was extracted from wild trees in the natural forest, very little wholesale deforestation took place in most parts of the basin, although rubber gatherers often chose to fell entire trees to extract all of their latex, rather than to "bleed" them sustainably. More damaging deforestation related to early agricultural efforts. A large section east of Belém called the Zona Bragantina was clear-cut to accommodate colonists from northeastern Brazil and, in growing numbers, from abroad. In western Amazonia, a combination of the search for rubber and pork-barrel politics resulted in the inauguration, in 1861, of what turned out to be a tragicomic half-century struggle to complete a railway between the town of Pôrto Velho, on the Rio Madeira, to Guajará-Mirim, at the western edge of Brazil on the Mamoré. With these two principal exceptions, rubber-era travel in Amazonia was by water. Roads, scarcely more than footpaths along the rivers' edges, were built to serve the region's growing population. Few but *seringueiros* (rubber gatherers) and Indian hunters or occasional farmers ventured away from shore and into the forests, which by and large remained pristine.

Socially, the end of the boom had major consequences. Weeds grew on the broad boulevards, and the opera houses in Manaus and in Belém shut down along with the collapse of commercial enterprise of all sorts. The big ships stopped coming from Europe and from the south. Between 1910 and 1920, Amazonia's population actually declined as rubber profiteers departed for safer havens elsewhere. Per capita income dropped from U.S. $323 in 1910 to only $74—barely more than what it had been in 1800—in 1920. Lights literally went out as electric power systems were switched off. And as the economy collapsed, so once again did Amazonia's morale. The anthropologist Charles Wagley, then of Columbia University, wrote in his classic 1953 study, *Amazon Town*: "The Amazon Valley, so prosperous and seemingly with such a brilliant future during the first decade of this century, became in a short time isolated and backward. A profound pessimism settled over the region."

Beneath the surface, the crash was in some respects a blessing. During the boom the *seringueiros* were dependent not only on cruel "barons" who controlled the land, but also on the urban middlemen called *aviadores* who managed the rubber trade and the credit system. The poverty that followed the crash also meant a degree of freedom for many Amazonian Indians and *caboclos* who had become more enslaved than enriched while the system endured. If it was to take another half-century for the lesson to sink in, the episode also revealed the extreme danger inherent in an extractive economy based entirely upon income from one single crop. What one scientist referred to as "the whole nightmare" had ended. Soon it would be time for "modern" technocracy to have its try at realizing the bright dreams of Wallace and Bates and Spruce and Agassiz.

CHAPTER 5

The Development Impulse

THERE WERE A "FULLY EQUIPPED HOSPITAL" AND A MODERN SCHOOL, a machine shop and a sawmill. A small railroad connected the site with a deep-water port. All dwellings featured such modern conveniences as filtered drinking water and shower baths—"just as unprecedented," according to one firsthand account, "as the mosquito netting." The planners of this city were doing far more than simply "pushing back the jungle." According to the *Bulletin of the Pan-American Union*, they "very early drew plans for schools and an entire town amply provided with parks, playgrounds, community recreation halls, and clubhouses, such as are generally regarded as outstanding features of modern small-city planning. Beautification of this city is also under way. Rapid progress is being made in the planting of trees to adorn the streets and the grading and development of lawns about the houses. Palms, eucalyptus, rubber, and mango trees now line most of the streets. An ornamental lighting system is being installed."

Is this an early description of Monte Dourado, the town on the Jari River that D. K. Ludwig, the headstrong American billionaire, began to construct in 1967? No. It is an account of a fascinating precursor: a long-discarded place

Henry Ford *(The Bettmann Archive)*

called Boa Vista that, more than forty years before, Henry Ford began to build near the mouth of the Tapajós River near Santarém. Soon after the Amazonian rubber boom collapsed, the far more efficient British and Dutch producers in Malaya established an OPEC-type mechanism to control rubber supplies and sustain prices at a level that consuming countries considered punitive. Outrage against the cartel became particularly vehement in the United States, by now the world's leading consumer. Thomas A. Edison was so concerned that he devoted the last years of his life to an unsuccessful search for a North American plant whose sap would end U.S. dependence on plantation rubber from Asia: Harvey Firestone established a rubber plantation in Liberia. Henry Ford, whose River Rouge plant was already producing a million cars a year by the mid-1920s, let it be known to his colleagues that he would fight the cartel "with all the strength and vigor that is in me." He reasoned that the optimum site for his own rubber plantation would be in the trees' native Amazonia. After painstaking research, Ford's men selected a Connecticut-sized stretch of land along the Tapajós, a southern tributary of the Amazon, some three hundred kilometers south of Santarém. In 1927 they struck a deal with the state, whereby it would receive seven percent of the profits after twelve years, in return for the concession to the company of all rights to the huge tract. Operations began late that year at what in Brazil soon became known as Fordlândia.

North Americans greeted the news with enthusiasm. "While there may be a difference of opinion as to the prospects of rubber growing in the Philippines and in Africa, there is none as to the Amazon Valley," crowed an October 1927 issue of a New York business magazine called *The Outlook*. "Brazil is the native home of the rubber plant, and the possibilities of extending production are almost unlimited." When land-clearing and construction began in 1928, however, progress was not altogether smooth. Company ships carrying supplies could not make the journey upriver from Santarém except during the high-water season, and there were resultant delays. Friction became intense between the Brazilian workers and their Yankee bosses over such matters as alcohol usage, and in 1928, two thousand of the three thousand men on the job were dismissed. Ford biographers Allan Nevins and Frank Ernest Hill stated in summary: "A new governor at the capital of Pará was making trouble, taxes were unpredictable and annoying, the Brazilian workers were dissatisfied to the point of revolt, and the planting and cultivation of seedlings was a perplexing and discouraging labor." By as late as 1932, with the United States now fully into the Depression and after $7 million had already been invested in the enterprise, less than seven thousand acres of land had been cleared. Many of the rubber seedlings that were planted soon died or became stunted. Not surprisingly, as we have seen, *Dothidella ulei* attacked many of those that survived. "The chief trouble," guessed Nevins and Hill, "seems to have been that the *Hevea* was a jungle tree, used to shelter, and when exposed in the open to pelting rains and long hot dry spells, could not survive."

What had so recently seemed a sure thing now became, at least to some observers, a dramatic gamble. "Henry Ford has never yet seen one of his big plans fail," intoned a German journalist who visited Brazil in 1932. "If this one succeeds, if the machine, the tractor, can open a breach in the great green wall of the Amazon jungle, if Ford plants millions of rubber trees where there used to be nothing but jungle solitude, then the romantic history of rubber will have a great new chapter. A new and titanic fight between nature and modern man is beginning." The company pushed on, attempting to export hardwoods harvested from cleared land while the first rubber-tree seedlings were passing through the six years of growth required before production could begin.

Ford made a second attempt at a different site on the Tapajós called Belterra, only sixty kilometers from the mouth of the Tapajós and far closer to Santarém and the world. The new property was acquired in 1934, in return for about a third of the original Boa Vista landholding; Fordlândia became an outlying "research station." Experiments with grafting and pesticides became at least partially effective. Between 1932 and 1941, the number of trees planted rose from 485,000 to more than 3.6 million. But in 1942 the harvest was still no more than a meager 750 tons of rubber—only a fraction of total Brazilian

Houses under construction at Belterra *(Henry Ford Museum)*

production that had reached 45,000 tons at the height of the boom, and an insignificant amount relative to wartime needs in the United States. Even at the end, after their investment had reached $20 million (a very large sum at the time), Ford officials were still insisting that the project would eventually work. In fact, they claimed, they had achieved far more, in far less time, than had the pioneer nineteenth-century planters in Asia. Despite these claims, Ford sold all of the Amazonian holdings to the Brazilian government in 1945. Soon weeds were creeping back onto the streets of Boa Vista, and the imported machinery began to rust.

Whether Ford's experiment provided conclusive proof about the viability of Amazonian rubber plantations remains debatable; the possibility that he might ultimately have succeeded cannot be denied. The fact is that after eighteen years he gave up. The story's significance, though, only begins with the symbolism of this defeat for a determined individual. In Amazonian history, from the time that the first hunter-gatherers followed the ancient large mammals into the lowlands, to the bitter end of the wild-rubber era, usage of the basin's resources had been almost exclusively extractive. The idea of making an *investment* was all but unheard of; one simply took or picked or dug up what was there, and carried the commodity off to market. Ford was the first person since Pombal to break the pattern and to bring to Amazonia the notion of economic development. His suggested route to El Dorado lay in the intensive application of capital and of the techniques of modern management and mass production that had put America on wheels. Decades later, when few but specialized historians had more than a vague memory of Fordlândia, such ideas about developing Amazonia would surface once again.

The Ford saga had another angle that was to recur often in the history of Brazil and Amazonia: he was the first major foreign investor to encounter nationalism there. The burst of economic liberalism that opened Amazonia to foreign ships as the rubber boom was maturing meant that the product moved to the markets mostly in foreign, not Brazilian, ships. Since much of the profit also ended up abroad, a nationalist reaction was inevitable. Populist military men, notably a young but already prominent *gaúcho* (southern Brazilian) officer-politician named Getúlio Vargas, seized the issue in the late 1920s and began to urge the importance to the nation of moving away from the Atlantic beaches and "occupying" the vast spaces to the north and west which were still all but empty. The importance for Brazil, Vargas stressed, was twofold. Colonization would protect the region from foreign incursions, and at the same time benefit vast numbers of peasants and settlers instead of only a few large landholders. More than a touch of spice was added to the Vargas brew by an Amazonian literary tradition, founded by the early-twentieth-century writer Euclides da Cunha and given later currency by Alberto Rangel in his famed 1914 novel *Inferno Verde* (Green Hell), that dwelt upon the region's impenetrability and the degree of "violation" already carelessly imposed by predatory humans.

President Getúlio Vargas

This mixture of drama, populism, and xenophobia, espoused by some Amazonian politicians as well as by security-minded military officers and fervent intellectuals, influenced various governors of Pará to turn against Ford and abet his departure from Brazilian agriculture. The idea of a nationalistic people's movement in Amazonia was reinforced in 1940 when Vargas, who three years before had seized power to become Brazil's dictator, delivered his notable "March to the West" speech. Successive stages of war and political turmoil were to defer any significant implementation of Vargas's vision until after he had committed suicide in 1954, bringing his second presidency to an abrupt end. But the dream was firmly planted, and would soon return to the top of the Brazilian agenda.

The president elected the following year, a charming and politically wily doctor named Juscelino Kubitschek, campaigned on a platform that stressed rapid economic progress. He promised "fifty years" of development during his five-year term, from 1955 to early 1961. Once in office, he did not delay in his efforts to make Brazil's dreams come true. He founded the national auto industry, built hydroelectric power plants and steel mills, and stimulated a wave of euphoria that even a sudden burst of inflation did little to dampen. His most flamboyant gesture was to resurrect a postscript to Brazil's first Constitution of 1824 that called for a capital, to be known as Brasília, to be constructed somewhere near the center of the country.

Locking hard on to this idea, Kubitschek hired two prominent architects, Lúcio Costa and Oscar Niemeyer, and mounted a crash program to build the new capital high on Brazil's central plateau and a full sixteen-hour drive northwest of the Rio de Janeiro beaches and nightspots that the politicians and federal bureaucrats preferred. Once Brasília was in place, Amazonia seemed far closer than it had from the distant coast. One speaker at the capital's inauguration even referred to it as "the launching pad for the conquest of Amazonia." Not surprisingly, then, it was also Kubitschek who began the construction of the first land link between the basin and the rest of Brazil— the 2,100-kilometer highway from Brasília to Belém. Before long, two million people had settled along this road, more than half of which had been pushed through dense tropical forest. Trucks and buses between the two points became crowded with goods and people. Amazonia was now integrated with the rest of the nation.

After Juscelino, Brazil once again fell into political disarray. His elected successor was Jânio Quadros, a probably brilliant but evidently unstable politician who picked as his laudable if quixotic goal the elimination of widespread corruption in government. Quadros remained in office for only six months, having logged record hours viewing Western films from a red velvet chair in the basement screening room in Brasília's ultramodern Planalto Palace as he vainly awaited corroboration from an apprehensive congress. Allegedly hoping

President Juscelino Kubitschek of Brazil raises the
first flag in Three Powers Plaza at the formal
installation of the national government in Brasília
on April 21, 1960. *(AP/Wide World Photos)*

that in the national interest he would be summoned back by popular demand,
he abdicated. But no such thing happened, and in 1961 the presidency passed
into the hands of his vice-president, João ("Jango") Goulart.

The primary shortcoming of President Goulart, who was widely accused of
being at least far too soft on the left if not a Communist himself, was not the
radicalism that the Brazilian military and U.S. advisers feared, but rather his
incompetence. Under Goulart's administration it did not take long for general
disorder to become even more commonplace than usual in volatile Brazil.
Along with shortages and strikes came a mighty burst of inflation that was
not to be exceeded until the early 1980s. Through it all, Goulart continued a
drumfire of demagogic appeals to the people; finally, the combination of real
and imagined dangers to the nation's stability persuaded reluctant military
officers that they had no alternative but to step in.

The brief coup, logistically abetted by the United States although as blood-
less as the one in which Dom Pedro II bowed out, began on March 31, 1964.
Goulart, along with many leftist politicians and academics, clandestinely left
Brazil. Into the presidency came a sternly moralistic general, Humberto Castello

Branco. Although he represented the so-called Sorbonne or intellectual wing of military thought, Castello Branco was deeply rooted in the Brazilian army's nationalist traditions as well. As his minister of planning he named a highly experienced technocrat and former Jesuit named Roberto Campos, who was so internationalist in his views, so eager to restore foreign investors' confidence in Brazil, that he became widely known by the English-language version of his name—Bobby Fields. The formula for rebuilding the Brazilian economy, Campos and most of the other economic planners of the period believed, lay in austerity measures to reduce runaway inflation (which would have reached an alleged 144 percent in 1964, had the trends established during the first three months of the year continued), and a large influx of private capital from abroad.

Conflicting attitudes toward Amazonia surfaced during this period. Many officers continued to favor the notion of "occupation" as a principle of national security. Here, after all, was half the entire country containing only four percent of its population (3.7 million people) and at the same time bordering no fewer than eight foreign countries. The threat of foreign domination of the Amazonian economy, even of political takeover, had always seemed to loom from North America and from Europe; now there was danger from the west as well. The recently elected president of Peru was an ineffectual but visionary architect named Fernando Belaúnde Terry, a Kubitschek-like figure whose principal goal was to link his nation with the rest of South America by means of a trans-Andean highway that he called the Carretera Marginal. The onset of this road's construction, which opened rich new lands on the eastern slopes of the Peruvian Andes, alarmed some of Brazil's generals. Other officers expressed concern about the findings of a book called *Amazonia and International Greed*, one of many strong-voiced works written by an Amazonian scholar named Artur César Ferreira Reis, who had also served as governor of the state of Amazonas.

In this book and other works, Reis claims not to hold any ideological bias, but merely to be making a "cold and dispassionate" analysis of a region that he finds to have been of consistent historical interest not just to scientists and naturalists but also to successive waves of greedy foreigners seeking to take advantage of Amazonia's traditional orientation toward Europe, North America, and the rest of Brazil. "Demographic pressures, pressures of hunger, pressures of economic interests involving the region's raw materials," Reis concludes, "can lead toward solutions that would be profoundly humiliating for Brazil. The perils surrounding Amazonia are looking us squarely in the eye." "*Integrar para não Entregar*"—integrate (the region) in order not to hand it over (to the foreigners)—became the catchy slogan of Brazil's domestic peace corps, which later sent missions deep into Amazonia.

Reis's warnings about foreign intentions were chilling to some of the army's senior officers. Others became enthusiastic about the prominent role in Brazilian economic development that Campos and his successors in the technocracies envisioned for the foreign private sector. To be sure, Campos was more in-terested in southern Brazil than in the Amazon. The foreign bankers and business leaders whom he entertained, often aboard a yacht belonging to the Mercedes-Benz chief executive in Brazil, had their gazes fastened not on Amazonia, but on the big markets developing in the large cities of central and southern Brazil, and on opportunities to found export-oriented industries in those areas. But Campos had his hopes for Amazonia as well. His model was a successful manganese-extraction operation on the island of Amapá, near the mouth of the river, that had been developed as a joint venture between Augusto de Azevedo Antunes, a highly respected business leader in Rio, and the Bethlehem Steel Corporation. As discoveries of large mineral deposits became known in the late 1960s, Campos saw potential for the development of the Amazonian mining and mineral sector on the basis—in large part—of foreign capital. Planners of the period also based their thinking on more traditional assumptions about the basin's potential for agriculture and cattle ranching, and for absorbing a growing segment of Brazil's fast-rising population. It was clear that Amazonia lagged well behind the rest of the nation in terms of per capita income, health, education, and almost any other index of social well-being. Regardless of underlying fears or motivations, a new concentration on the region's rapid development seemed, finally, a logical basic element in the program of national revitalization that the military held as its mission.

Evidence of the keen if ambivalent new interest in the region soon began to emerge. In 1965 President Castello Branco declared "Operation Amazonia." Over the next several years the ministries issued numerous laws and decrees that, it was hoped, would move the region vigorously forward. Under the succeeding presidency of Artur da Costa e Silva, a tough barracks-room soldier who took over and strengthened the office in 1967, the program continued. A decadent old agency was dusted off and in 1968 was renamed the Super-intendency for the Development of Amazonia (SUDAM), with broad powers to hand out tax incentives and provide easy credit for investors in agriculture or industry. The idea was not only to build Pará and eastern Amazonia, but to foster "poles of development" sprinkled across the basin. This was the principle that lay behind the revival of an old program, with roots in Amazonia's nineteenth-century internationalism, wherein the region around Manaus was established as a free-trade zone. The decree provided incentives for creating export-oriented assembly industries in the very center of the basin, as well as for agriculture and ranching, and the clear hope was that foreign firms would become major participants.

Although Brazil's leaders in the late 1960s paid little official attention to the idea of small-farmer colonization of Amazonia (or agriculture anywhere in the country, for that matter), one of their accomplishments during the period nurtured a spontaneous new wave of it. This was the improvement and completion of a road, begun by Juscelino Kubitschek as the east-west counterpart of the Belém–Brasília Highway, linking the town of Cuiabá, in the state of Mato Grosso, with Pôrto Velho, in what was then the almost totally unoccupied territory of Rondônia. In September 1966 I traveled the length of this newly passable highway in the company of General Vernon Walters, then serving as U.S. military attaché in the U.S. Embassy. What I wrote at the time reflects the sense of hope and promise that was then attached to the opening of new Amazonian lands:

> Northwestward from Cuiabá proceeds one of the world's more remarkable roads: 877 miles of red dirt, hacked by machete and bulldozer through arid *sertão* (desert) and dense jungle to Pôrto Velho on the Madeira River. This road, first opened in 1960 but only now starting to bring results, has opened to southern Brazil a whole new region—Acre and Rondônia—for colonization and development. At places it has become a smooth highway along which a Jeep pickup can travel smoothly at fifty-five miles an hour. More often—particularly during the rainy season—long stretches turn into mud and ten miles an hour is a spine-jolting speed. Between the two towns the road meets four rivers that must be forded by barge, and engineers have built some 130 other bridges across smaller creeks and ravines. When the bridges flood out or rot (most are of wood), a truck or car must make perilous detours through the rivers themselves.
>
> The road was hastily slashed into being during the final months of former president Juscelino Kubitschek's regime. Kubitschek had already completed the north-south Belém–Brasília Highway. To complete a gigantic "Southern Cross" of pioneering roads, Juscelino dreamed of adding the final stretches needed to link the Atlantic Ocean with Brazil's wildest west. He got the job done, but so sloppily that the jungle started to reclaim it as soon as he had left office. Fleeing brawlers and bandits along the highway burned the bridges (this still happens), and the trip became at times a two-week nightmare. But last year the Brazilian army created a special engineering battalion to rebuild the road. Spread out across a distance of more than a thousand miles, surely one of the lengthiest deployments of a single battalion anywhere in the world, these soldiers have already recuperated much of the road.
>
> Beyond such Mato Grosso towns as Diamantino and Rosario, civilization starts petering out. Northwestern Mato Grosso becomes a vast brown plain with literally nothing on it. Then comes primitive Rondônia, whose soil is rich and where the road has made possible a strenuous new wave of colonization. Brought by trucks belonging to colonization companies in Brazil's south, the colonists take over land that they provide, and have access to some long-term financing from the companies. They jump off a truck, build a primitive little house, and start clearing jungle. Sometimes they are attacked by Indians. Sometimes the mosquitoes are so thick they must clothe themselves

from head to toe despite the hundred-plus-degree heat. It is a world of bare subsistence, for as yet there is no market for their crops. They hunt for much of their food. But these new pioneers come to Rondônia because the land is very cheap (almost free). And, with the road, the opportunity is good.

Ten to fifteen trucks, many of them carrying immigrants, reach the border of Rondônia from Mato Grosso each day. The territory's population, only 37,000 in 1950, has now topped 100,000. Along the road new towns are cropping up and the few old ones are mushrooming. The settlement called Rondônia, for example, was a ghost town until the road was built. It had served only as an isolated telegraph station and as recently as 1953 there were only four houses there. Now the municipality contains about six thousand people, and more pour in every day. This year the town's first bar opened. Its owner, an immigrant from the northeast named Cícero Fernandes, arrived about a year and a half ago. He set up a small dry-goods store, started trading in rubber, then waited for progress. It came fast. "My business has doubled in the last year," he says. "The road has been the difference. The truckdriver comes through here on his way to São Paulo and I place my order. In just two weeks, he's back." At the rate Brazil grows, it seems likely that Cícero will have a ten-story building alongside his thriving commercial house in a decade or so.

Pôrto Velho has become, according to one citizen, "a boomtown that hasn't yet had time to figure out that it is one." What has hit there, in addition to the road and a modest revival in the old rubber-gathering business, is a mineral rush resulting from the discovery, in about 1952, of substantial nearby quantities of cassiterite or tin ore. The result is that Pôrto Velho has been transformed from a sleepy old river town, left over from another era, into a lively, brawling frontier capital. "Spit neither on the floor, nor on the walls, nor beside the bed," read the rules on the always full-up—if still sloppy and broken-down and old—Pôrto Velho Hotel. Its thriving terrace bar is full late into the evening with newly rich tin miners, pilots, truckdrivers, and businessmen. When several of us walked into a whorehouse about 11:00 P.M. and found the place all but empty, the madam bustled up and apologized. "You should have come earlier," she said. "All our young ladies are occupied." Pôrto Velho and Rondônia, in short, are no longer the end of the world.

This was the kind of story that, at any time since the mid-1960s, was there to be told about one part of Amazonia or another. Many planners felt that Rondônia represented a widely replicable model. The stirrings there, however, were not what prompted the real surge of roadbuilding and human settlement in Amazonia that was to begin in 1970. In June of that year President Emílio Garrastazu Médici, who assumed the presidency after Costa e Silva's death, made a routine visit to the impoverished northeast and was shocked by what he saw. His response was to think that Amazonia could be a cure for the region's problems, and that the best way to bring about the redemption would be to build a road so that northeasterners could escape and diffuse into "fertile" Amazonia. His administration, he said, would offer "land without men for men without land."

The government, Médici announced, would construct a new pioneering east-west highway that would run through ("open up") the heart of the Amazon from east to west—from the town of Marabá on the Tocantins River, due south of Belém, clear across to Benjamin Constant on the Solimões at the border with Colombia. Accompanying Médici's roadbuilding scheme, tellingly called the Program of National Integration (PIN), was a plan for INCRA, the colonization agency, to be revitalized. Its principal task would be to settle one million families at selected spots along the highway where it was felt that good farming conditions existed. In Brasília the agency's planners, few of whom had firsthand knowledge of Amazonia, set about this task with admirable bureaucratic precision. They laid grids across the track of the highway and decided that every so often there would be an *"agrovila"* or an *"agrópolis"* or a *"rurópolis,"* each with a predetermined number of people and schools and teachers and doctors and nurses and hospital beds. Marabá itself was one of the focal points. A second was Itaituba on the Tapajós, not far from where Ford's plantations had been. A third site was Altamira on the Xingu River, roughly halfway between the two others. Seventy-five percent of the colonists were supposed to come from the Northeast, which at the time represented only 13 percent of Brazil's gross product but 30 percent of the population.

Construction of the Trans-Amazon began, after presumably thorough planning, no more than two weeks after Médici's announcement. The government would lay claim to all land lying one hundred kilometers on either side of the road, and INCRA would parcel one-hundred-hectare lots out to colonists at the target locations. Easy credit terms, access to health and education, technical assistance, and other major incentives were offered. But even with all these advantages, the program turned out to bear little resemblance to the heady success of the early rush into Rondônia. There was malaria at Marabá. Poor soils impeded progress around Itaituba, whose small farms, when I saw them in 1983, seemed still not to be producing beyond the subsistence level, despite heavy deforestation. Although relatively good soils were to be found around Altamira, unexpectedly large parts of the region were also found to be highly infertile. When the lands were opened, moreover, those who took the best advantage of them were not the migrant northeasterners for whom the whole program was designed, but the Amazonian *caboclos* who had been there all along. Those northeasterners who did find their way to Altamira (only 31 percent of all colonists there, according to one survey) had to learn agricultural techniques that were brand-new to them, and the promised technical assistance often failed to materialize. During the rainy season it was not possible to keep

Road maintenance in
Amazonia—usually difficult
(Roger D. Stone)

An Amazon town, Tucuruí, during the flood season *(Roger D. Stone)*

the road open. Basic supplies were often lacking. Although local officials were well aware of these and other problems, reported the anthropologist Emilio Moran of Indiana University, who spent much time there, the word somehow never got back to Brasília, and the necessary adjustments simply did not get made.

In all, only 7,839 families were established in the three model colonies during the seven years from the beginning of Médici's program until 1977, relative to a goal of fully 100,000 families by 1974. Had the emphasis on colonization been sustained, some greater measure of success might eventually have been achieved in the INCRA areas, although this form of activity is clearly no cure for broad population pressures. "If the PIN had been executed as planned," wrote the sociologists Charles H. Wood and John Wilson, "the program would have absorbed 3.8 percent of the rural to urban flow in the 1960s and 3.0 percent of the movement in 1970s." But Brasília's span of attention had long since been exceeded, and objectives other than human settlement were now paramount. "Historically," says Robert F. Skillings, who ran the World Bank's Brazilian loan portfolio at the time, "it was in about 1974 that attention shifted from the small farmer in Amazonia to the commercial enterprise. This was the moment of general disenchantment with the Trans-Amazon and the resettlement programs. By the time the Médici government ended and General [Ernesto] Geisel came to power, they wanted to sweep the place clean. I can remember João Paulo dos Reis Veloso, the Minister of Planning at the time, saying very frankly that things had not worked out very well in small farming, and that he had to make Amazonia give us production on a commercial scale. He said that the only way to do that would be to work with big enterprise." Veloso was, of course, motivated in large part by the heavy pressure of the "oil shock" of late 1973, when the petroleum producers of the Middle East quadrupled their prices. Since Brazil imported 70 percent of its oil, enormous increases in export earnings would be required.

The mid-1970s, then, became the time of unprecedented interest in the crash development of the Amazon for the benefit not of the poor, but of large-scale Brazilian and foreign entrepreneurs. Roadbuilding continued: the highway from Cuiabá in Mato Grosso to Santarém, a road from Manaus seven hundred kilometers north to Venezuela, the beginnings of what was known as the Perimetral Norte, another east-west link that would do for the northern part of the basin what the Trans-Amazon would do for the south. But the emphasis had shifted from public to private investment to generate export income, and whatever fear of foreign dominance the generals harbored was submerged in the sudden new impulse for crash development. SUDAM frenziedly approved hundreds of big cattle projects. The rate of Amazonian deforestation rose sharply as these entrepreneurs cleared vast stretches of virgin forest for their animals. INCRA, too, increased the rate of its land distribution to relatively large-scale farmers. Manaus, equipped with a new international airport that opened in 1976, enjoyed a giddy boom based on its assembly plants and on the fact that visitors from Brazil's south could go there, purchase stereos and television sets, carry them home on the four-hour airplane flights to Rio de Janeiro or São Paulo, and still come out ahead. Although it lacked the special advantages that Manaus enjoyed, Belém moved toward becoming the first Amazonian city with a population of a million. The basin's population, less than two million in 1940 and 3.6 million in 1960, already seemed likely to reach at least eight million by 1985.

A few companies, in response, were now beginning to make the first significant private foreign investments in Amazonia since the 1950s, when Bethlehem Steel joined Antunes in the manganese venture at Amapá. Companies such as Volkswagen and the King Ranch found the SUDAM incentives irresistible and founded cattle ranches along the Belém–Brasília Highway in southern Pará. Major mining and mineral investments were undergoing active consideration. The most dramatic foreign presence in Amazonia during the mid-1970s was, beyond a doubt, that of Daniel K. Ludwig and his development scheme along the Jari River that flows into the lower Amazon from the north. Ludwig, who had become a billionaire in the shipping business, had in the

The plantation at Jari, formerly owned by the American entrepreneur D. K. Ludwig. The photograph shows the sharp difference between the natural forest (left) and the tidy rows of pulpwood across the road. *(Photograph by Loren McIntyre © National Geographic Society, 1980)*

1960s begun a worldwide search for a place to make a major pulp and paper investment. After a false start in Africa, Ludwig received a warm reception from Roberto Campos when he turned to Brazil in 1967. Within a short time he had quietly (the nationalist reaction was to come later) arranged to acquire, for $3 million, a tract of land along the Jari—a plot close to double the size of Henry Ford's million-hectare Fordlândia.

At Jari, Ludwig planned an investment of some $300 million in a complex that would have three principal activities: to mine a substance called kaolin, used in the manufacture of porcelain and in plentiful supply on the behemoth landholding; to grow rice on the fertile *várzea* lands bordering the river; and to exploit the area's timber resources through sales both of sawn wood and of pulp. This was the heart of the often-told Jari story, for none of it would ever have happened had Ludwig not, in the 1950s, become convinced that the world was facing a major fiber shortage. He then looked for a fast-growing pulpwood tree that would ease the shortage and make him millions as well. It was his discovery in 1965 of the *gmelina* tree, a native of India and Burma, that triggered his search for a place to put it. Jari was secured in 1967 and the first *gmelina* was in the ground soon after the closing. *Gmelina* plantation difficulties had already surfaced by the early 1970s, and a slower-growing but more durable plywood species, the Caribbean pine, was added to the mix. A few observers were already beginning to warn that Jari was headed for a Ford-type debacle. But world pulp prices rose sharply between 1973 and 1975, and in early 1976 Ludwig made the fateful decision to order a $269 million pulp mill from a Japanese manufacturer and have it towed across the Pacific, through the Panama Canal, and up the Amazon. There it arrived in early 1978—a dramatic symbol of the most audacious industrial project ever attempted anywhere in Amazonia.

Amazingly, Ludwig's scheme paled in comparison to the frenzied ideas that were by the mid-1970s percolating in the minds of Brazil's master planners. The nation's "economic miracle"—five years of heady economic growth between 1968 and 1973, when the first oil-price hike sent Brazil's economy reeling—had led to a new and exuberant burst of nationalist zeal. The nation would finally, Brazilians and their leaders came to agree, achieve its rightful status as a great power. Domestic natural resources were, after all, at least comparable in most respects to those held by the two great powers. If Brazil lacked oil, cars would run on sugar alcohol, and development of the nation's ample hydroelectric potential would power the industrial surge. Fast-growing exports of minerals, manufactured goods, and agricultural products would, they hoped, more than pay for Arab petroleum. Antonio Delfim Netto, the chubby professor who guided Brazil's burgeoning economy, became a national hero. If severe economic problems were looming ahead, Delfim could still talk glibly of accelerating around the corners as the perpetual "land of tomorrow" raced flat out toward the Nirvana of *Grandeza* that it had been pursuing for centuries.

Construction (as a possibly quixotic joint venture with tiny Paraguay) began in 1974 on the giant Itaipu hydroelectric project, which by the 1990s is scheduled to be the world's largest, with an installed capacity of 12,600 megawatts, and was budgeted at no less than $14 billion. Brazilians began to grow soybeans, historically all but unheard of there, and production soon rose to second place behind the United States. Somewhat to its own surprise, Brazil found markets for frozen chicken in the Middle East, and for its eighteen-passenger Bandeirante commuter turboprop in a variety of countries including the United States. Prices soared at restaurants and nightclubs in Rio and São Paulo, where newly rich businessmen vied to discover the oldest and most expensive Scotch whiskey. Foreign banks and investors, emboldened by the relative stability that had settled over the Brazilian economy as a result of the austerity and inflation-reduction program of the late 1960s, cast aside long-standing suspicions and judged Brazil to be an acceptable "risk." *Grandeza*'s leading symbol was Angra I, the white-elephant nuclear power station and Brazil's long-awaited entry into the nuclear age, which was completed in 1983 on the pearly sand of the beach near Angra dos Reis on the coast south of Rio de Janeiro.

The principal role that the master planners now perceived for Amazonia had to do neither with colonization nor with cattle raising, which by the mid-1970s was also beginning to look unpromising when practiced on deforested Amazonian heartland. Though Roberto Campos was long since out of office, successors pursued his early dream: mining and mineral resources, whose quantities rivaled those of the USSR and the United States, would be the principal elements in the future development of the basin. The manganese operation at Amapá would be only the beginning. At the Serra dos Carajás in southern Pará, over which pilots had long reported magnetic disturbances that caused compass aberrations, U.S. Steel geologists in 1967 discovered what turned out to be the world's largest deposit of high-grade iron ore. You did not even have to dig for this ore—it was right there on the surface, eighteen billion tons of it. Along the Trombetas River, a northern tributary of the lower Amazon, bauxite had been found in the 1950s. Nickel, tin, copper, and other minerals were also available in commerical quantity and quality. Prospectors were finding gold along many of the rivers. Brazilian officials rejected the grandiose idea, proposed by the American futurist Herman Kahn soon after the 1964 coup, of damming the lower Amazon to generate electricity and turn Amazonia into the Great Lakes of the Southern Hemisphere. Even in the absence of such a monumental public work, engineers estimated Amazonia's hydroelectric power potential to be at least 70,000 megawatts—a supply sufficient even for the intensive manufacture of alumina and aluminum, which requires vast amounts of energy.

By the onset of the 1980s, it had all crystallized into the grandest Amazonian development scheme of all: the so-called Grande Carajás program. This integrated effort would encompass fully 90 million hectares in the state of Pará and in the neighboring states of Goiás and Maranhão on the periphery of Amazonia, and would include agricultural, ranching, and urban-development components to complement the keystone mining projects. The core of the program would be the iron mine at the Serra dos Carajás. A total investment of $5.3 billion there would inaugurate the mining operation and also finance the construction of an 890-kilometer railway through the forest that would carry the ore to a new port to be built at São Luís, the island capital of the state of Maranhão. Also at São Luís, Alcoa (with Shell as a minority partner) would construct a maxi refining and smelting complex, using bauxite from the Trombetas deposits. Copper, nickel, and manganese mining operations would be launched. Power would be supplied by means of the world's fourth largest hydroelectric complex, at Tucuruí on the Tocantins River, with a total planned capacity of eight million kilowatts and a $5 billion price tag. Agricultural and cattle-raising ventures would be built for the fast-rising populations that these activities would attract, and an elaborate infrastructure of towns, roads, airports, and other facilities was proposed.

As these plans were taking shape, the trickle of people into Rondônia that I had observed in the 1960s had turned into an uncontrolled torrent of such magnitude that Brazil, *Grandeza* notwithstanding, was once again being forced to think about organizing an effort to assist small farmers moving into the frontier areas of the northwest. The reason was not any particular increase in the flow of people from the northeast, but rather overcrowding in the rural south. Throughout the twentieth century, successive waves of immigrants— from Italy, Poland, Germany, the Ukraine, Japan, Korea—had flowed into the southern Brazilian states of Rio Grande do Sul and Paraná. There they had planted coffee and vegetables and wheat, and run cattle for meat and milk and cheese. For several generations these farms and the families on them had prospered. But by the 1970s the south was becoming overcrowded. Young families could not economically farm the ever-smaller tracts they were inheriting from the previous generation. For many the solution was to escape, and the easiest route was north and west into the virgin lands of Amazonia. The northwest region, encompassing part of the state of Mato Grosso and the entire federal territory of Rondônia, is three-quarters the size of France. The early migrations of the 1960s had barely made a dent, and the tide rose fast as the 1970s progressed.

Some began to refer to it as the Brazilian equivalent of the occupation of the western United States. Over the decade the region's population passed one million people and, at last count, was growing at a rate of 10.8 percent a year (a whopping 15.8 percent a year in Rondônia). No end was in sight: in

1977, 6,000 people crossed the frontier into Rondônia at the town of Vilhena; the equivalent figure for 1980 was 58,000. The government was faced with a difficult decision. It could simply ignore the northwest and let its colonists fight unassisted against a complex of deep problems ranging from malaria to disputed land titles and violence, from bad transportation to the lack of technical assistance. These were farmers accustomed to temperate and not tropical latitudes, and they were therefore trying to learn new agricultural technologies in totally primitive conditions with almost no effective technical assistance. In view of these realities, the government's alternative was to wink at its own stated emphasis on large-scale entrepreneurship and dig into an already emptying exchequer to find financial support for an organized colonization effort.

The decision, reached in 1981 by the government of President João Baptista Figueiredo, was to ignore the failures of the early 1970s, follow the traditional philosophy suggesting that "occupation" is good—and go with the flow. The government that year moved to create an intensive colonization program, to be called Polonoroeste (Northwest Pole) at a total projected cost of more than U.S. $1.5 billion. Highway 364, as the Cuiabá–Pôrto Velho Highway was now known, would be paved to facilitate transportation and market access even during the rainy season, when the dirt roads of Amazonia often become impassable. Feeder roads would reach deep into the forest from the main highway, and colonies to be assisted by INCRA would be established along them. Far more than subsistence agriculture was envisioned, for studies showed that the region had potential for coffee, cocoa, and even rubber plantations. The World Bank became interested and, after receiving Brazilian reassurances that the integrated program would contain elements of protection for the regions eight thousand Indians as well as an environmental conservation component, came in with more than $400 million in loans for Polonoroeste—its largest ever for a Brazilian project.

In a recent interview, Nils Tcheyan, a World Bank official who had much to do with the loan package for Northwest Brazil, cited evidence of progress in the region. By 1984 the highway was sufficiently improved, he said, to remain open all twelve months. The flow of commerce in both directions was far smoother than it had been during the roughest pioneer days. The government's ability to provide technical support was improving, and in chronically unhealthy Rondônia the fear of malaria had disappeared from smaller towns as well as from Pôrto Velho. Indian reserves were demarcated and *posseiros* (squatters) were being removed, although the overall progress of the Indian-protection program has been less than fully satisfactory. Tcheyan reserved his highest praise for the gritty and determined character of the migrants participating in the program. "All the farmers there are capable of going beyond the subsistence level," he said. "They prefer the perennial crops, where there is real money to be made. The soil is good and technical assistance is coming in. Mostly, there is simply the spirit and the energy of the people. It's amazing when you go out there into the interior, where there is nothing, no hotels, and where you're completely dependent on people's willingness to take you into their homes. Invariably they will give you their food even if there's none left over for them, move you into the principal bedroom in the house and sleep somewhere else, tell you about their plans and accomplishments. They are tough and just wonderful, and even though the circumstances are difficult, they give you a feeling of confidence in their future and the future of the region."

Polonoroeste is designed to accommodate directly the influx of 12,000 families, or 60,000 people, a year into the northwest, and indirectly aid the far wider circle of those already there or arriving spontaneously to pursue activities other than farming. But even a project of this magnitude and financial commitment pales beside mammoth Grande Carajás. And it is this Herculean effort that has captured the imagination (if no more than a fraction of the required financial resources) of Brazil and the world. Several years ago Brazilian bureaucrats, businessmen, and bankers launched aggressive efforts to attract public and private capital, from all over the world, to the Carajás project. Its total dimensions were daunting. By 1990, the plan called for no less than $70 billion in total public and private investment; the value of Carajás exports, authorities confidently predicted, would reach $15 billion—ten times what all of Brazil's exports had been only twenty-five years before. Grande Carajás would support no fewer than 1.5 million jobs.

These grand ideas were taking shape, however, just as high interest rates and poor conditions in the world economy were beginning to cause severe problems in Brazil as elsewhere. The debt, once regarded as a logical handmaiden of the quest for *Grandeza*, had become a monster approaching $100 billion by 1984, and often, with world markets soft, the only way to service it was to borrow more. As the debt mounted, the inflation rate, stimulated in part by a system of automatic indexation once perceived as an ingenious innovation, soared well past the previous peaks, achieved just before the military coup of 1964, toward the unprecedented level of more than 200 percent. Unemployment mounted. Crime reached new heights as hungry people sacked supermarkets in São Paulo and Rio de Janeiro and snatched purses, wallets, and jewelry on the streets. Accusations of corruption in high places, and of glaring inefficiencies in the giant state-owned companies, become commonplace at home and abroad. Though the International Monetary Fund demanded and was accorded severe austerity measures as a means of restoring economic order in Brazil, there was talk also of defaulting on the debt as an alternative to sacrificing the redemocratization (*abertura*) that had become a national goal.

By the mid-1980s Brazil's gross national product was back to about where it had been in 1975. Though indirect presidential elections were announced for 1985 and the Figueiredo government was already perceived as a lame duck, the future remained uncertain. Speculation continued as to whether the military would really surrender power, even after more than twenty years of increasingly ineffective governance. Some predicted a popular revolution or some other traumatic event; hundreds of thousands took to the streets in support of direct elections. But as disarray again grew in Brazil, few changes were made at the top. "The crisis continues," said Delfim Netto, now the villain. "And so does Delfim." The planners were still calling for "adjustment" to be accompanied by export-oriented growth.

In Amazonia, the crisis meant slowdowns at all of the Grandes Projetos, and only the northwest colonization scheme, with its financing from the World Bank, remained on schedule. But if there were stretch-outs and postponements, there was also no time in Brazilian history when a quick economic return from Amazonia would be of greater benefit to the nation as a whole.

CHAPTER 6

Students of the Forest

RICHARD O. ("ROB") BIERREGAARD, A BROAD-SHOULDERED ORNITHOL-ogist, walks sweating along a narrow path in a ten-hectare patch of rain forest seventy kilometers north of Manaus. I follow. Although occasional shafts of sunlight pierce through the multiple layers of canopy all the way to the forest floor, the light is that of early evening. There is silence in the forest except for occasional cries by the aptly-named Screaming Piha. Then Bierregaard makes a birdcall himself. An answer comes from a colleague and we move toward the sound. Soon we arrive at a line of mist nets strung, badminton-court height, between the tree trunks. Deftly, Bierregaard extracts from the net a small brown bird lying quietly enmeshed in it. "Female woodcreeper," he mutters. He weighs and bands the bird, then places it on its back in his palm. It lies still, legs in the air. Then he turns it onto its stomach and it quickly flies off, almost instantly disappearing from view.

The woodcreeper is one of seventeen thousand bird catches that Bierregaard and his field crews had, as of mid-1983, made in some fifteen forest patches of various sizes. All are located north of Manaus, on land conceded by the local development agency, SUFRAMA, to farmers and entrepreneurs intent

After the burn *(Roger D. Stone)*

on clearing and burning the virgin forest to make cattle pastures. In 1977 this forest contained large cats and troops of monkeys, stately macaws and hundreds of other colorful bird species. Now the cats and the monkeys and many of the birds have gone from the 50 percent of the lands that, by law, the ranchers must retain as forest. Where the land has been cleared, it looks—as Bierregaard puts it—like "our Mount St. Helens." Blackened tree trunks are scattered like giant jackstraws across the scorched earth. Even though the burn had taken place three months before, only a few timid shoots of green had pushed through the dry, crusted red earth.

Soon after he arrived in 1979, Bierregaard began to collect baseline data on birds from undisturbed forest patches. Information about each bird went first onto a three-by-five file card. Later it was inserted into an Apple II computer in the air-conditioned bedroom of Bierregaard's house in the Parque Dez section of Manaus. After forest-cutting began, Bierregaard could return to the same sections of forest previously surveyed and measure them for losses of bird species due to shrinking territories, food-supply problems, or other forms of disturbance. In one ten-hectare patch, the number of species found in Bierregaard's nets dropped from seventy to forty after only six months. Isolated forest patches only one hectare in size are, says Bierregaard, "so devoid of species that it's hardly worth netting them anymore."

Why is Bierregaard working in such a disrupted environment when he could find, at no great distance from Manaus, pristine conditions not very different

Lee Harper, a member of the "Minimum Critical Size" staff, shows a bird mist-netted as part of research project. *(Roger D. Stone)*

from those surveyed by Bates or Spruce? For one thing, the World Wildlife Fund and Brazil's National Institute for Amazon Development (INPA), the co-sponsors of Bierregaard's work, want to establish how large an Amazonian forest resource or national park need be if it is to retain all of its species. "Today there is a very ambitious program of national park development in Amazonia," says Thomas E. Lovejoy, vice-president for science at World Wildlife Fund– U.S. "The question is whether the new parks that have been created are big enough to do the job of protecting the species for which they were designed. There is a theory that 250,000 hectares or more may be required if everything in a given section of Amazonia is to be preserved. It will take a good many years to get the data—we are hoping that the project will last for twenty— but at the end of it we hope to have good answers about what happens when you scale down from there." A broader objective of the project, Bierregaard adds, is to test a scientific theory called island biogeography. According to this theory, it is inevitable that biological losses will occur when a natural area is made to shrink or when a landmass once attached to a mainland becomes isolated. The doctrine also holds that, generally speaking, a large island should be able to support more species than a series of small islands of the same total area—and that the principle should also apply to large and small patches in the tropical forest. About this point, however, there has been some controversy.

"Lovejoy was sitting around one day back in 1975," says Bierregaard. "There had been a big flurry of island biogeography papers published, including one by Simberloff in which he said that island biogeography theory is actually neutral when it comes to whether you would have more species in a large number of small areas or in a smaller number of larger areas. A lot of people misread him and thought he was advocating small reserves that would probably be inadequate for conservation. It all became quite a *cause célèbre* in the literature. A lot of people jumped on it right away and talked about the dangers in the argument, but nobody had any real data, and the real question was how to get some. Tom knew of the law here that said half the land had to be left in forest. He started wondering whether he could do a giant experiment by rearranging some of this 50 percent into a series of 'islands' of different sizes, and then measuring the consequences. In 1977 he came to INPA and worked out a plan, and then he came back to the States and asked if I'd like to learn a new language.

"I finally got here in 1979 and have been plugging away at it ever since. What we've got now is one of the largest ecological experiments that's ever been perpetrated. What's important about it is the amount of control we have. You can learn a lot about a system just by going in and counting trees or banding birds or whatever, but you can learn a lot more if you systematically disturb it a little and see what happens. So we've been running around for four years now, marking off areas, sometimes trying to guess where the farmer's going to cut next, setting up areas of one and ten and one hundred and one thousand hectares. We gather pre-isolation data for a variety of organisms, to get a good picture of what we have in our test tubes before we change the heat. Then, using the same techniques, we keep on measuring as isolation proceeds."

Over the four years of the project's existence, some forty Brazilian and foreign scientists have gathered data on behalf of what in Brazil is known as the Biological Dynamics of Forest Fragments experiment (which the Brazilian press has called, more succinctly, the Projeto Lovejoy). Snakes, frogs, small mammals, army ants and various other insects, soils, palms, microclimates, and bats have all been surveyed with varying degrees of success. Some of the scientists have left, frustrated. A Smithsonian Institution zoologist, Louise Emmons, found it all but impossible to find small quadrupeds on the forest floor, and she quit, later to establish a study of jaguars and other large predators in the out-of-the-way Manu National Park in the Peruvian Amazon. Living conditions have been primitive in the field camps, and some of the study areas have been far from healthy. Ailments including amoebic dysentery and a particularly unpleasant disease called leishmaniasis have afflicted workers on the project. (This last, transmitted by one variety of sand fly, erodes ears and noses in its latter stages; the only known cure is massive doses of antimony injected

through a flashlight-sized syringe.) Yet Bierregaard's is far from the sole element of the project that is already producing solid accomplishment. Another
of its highly active dimensions is the tree survey work being carried out by
Judy Rankin, a skilled and determined botanist and ecologist with a University
of Michigan doctorate.

Judy Rankin, botanist and ecologist, discusses specimens with visitors to
"Minimum Critical Size" project field site. *(Roger D. Stone)*

Working in six reserve clusters and on fifteen separate sites, Rankin and her
field assistants had by mid-1983 inspected and tagged 28,000 trees of at least
ten centimeters in diameter. "Aside from finding out just who is out there and
what the distribution patterns are," says Rankin, "we are looking into whether
our reserves actually represent the woody flora of the region as a whole. We
are interested in populations as well as in species. And with survey techniques
that reflect population structure, we can look at what happens to a population
when it is cut up into subpopulations." Rankin and her assistants, often young
scientists learning the basics of tropical forest ecology before moving on to
graduate schools, have also been studying such phenomena as the establishment
of seedlings and their growth rates; the effect of naturally caused treefalls; and
the process that Rankin calls "secondarization"—the demographic changes
that occur at the edge of the forest after it has been isolated because of altered
wind, moisture, and sunlight conditions. While seedlings of some species
wither and die with heightened solar radiation, other plants such as the cecropia

thrive at the forest edge and tend to predominate for the short term. During later stages of succession, some of the original forest species make a slow comeback.

Bierregaard wonders about how finely tuned the project's ultimate conclusions can ever be: "We've established controls over space and time, and we have deliberately limited our variables. If each of our reserves had different soil types, for instance, it would be hard to generalize the results. Even so, at the end we won't be able to say that the minimum critical size—the point at which there would be no species loss at all—is precisely 237,004 hectares. We know that we don't expect ten-hectare units to be effective for conservation. The one-hundred-hectare size, though, will preserve some portion of the biota. Obviously the large predators will go. You won't have any jaguars or large eagles in there. But quite a few groups of howler monkeys could fit into a one-hundred-hectare patch, and seven or eight mixed-species bird flocks could survive in there. You're also dealing with an area that's realistic; fly over the forest and you see that lots of one-hundred-hectare patches are being left around. We'll be able to replicate our data at the one-hundred-hectare level, and now we are lucky to have our first area of one thousand hectares. It's so hilly and full of *igarapés* that the rancher doesn't really want to clear it, and we have the longest string of pre-isolation data from there that we've ever collected. Still, the scale of one thousand hectares is so big that here we're almost getting beyond what we can measure."

Rankin, too, remains cautious about the results to date. "This is an experimental project," she says, "and the only one of its kind. So far, we've been able at least to establish control areas so that we can observe these organisms doing whatever nature intended them to do when this huge disturbance of isolation takes place. That takes time." She speaks about the "horrible" problem she faces in identifying the plants she collects. Most specimens enter the lab bereft of flowers or fruit, which are easier to classify than leaves; and the advances in Amazonian plant taxonomy are currently so rapid that yesterday's positive identification is often today's guess. The sheer variety of species in the tropical forest further complicates matters. "We go out and decide what we think is a biological species based on field experience," she says. "But people are revising all the families, and some genera are simply going to disappear." She faces myriad other obstacles. Since some Brazilian scientists seem reluctant to work in the field, by and large preferring to keep their feet to the fire in capitals and major universities or research centers, Rankin relies mainly on foreigners who do not always adapt easily to conditions in Amazonia. Thanks largely to her secondary role as administrator of INPA's graduate program, she faces stacks of paperwork in her Manaus office that frequently keep her busy for weeks on end. And there are endless problems with the project's field vehicles, which all possess wonderfully reliable Mercedes truck engines but whose bodies are not up to the pounding they take on the washboard dirt roads leading out of Manaus.

Still, the young and difficult project has already begun to produce tangible results. Listen, for instance, to Bierregaard talking about just one set of observations in one isolated ten-hectare area: "At the time of isolation there were three troops of monkeys in there—tamarins, howlers, and a pair of bearded sakis. At first they didn't seem to be having too much of a problem. But after a couple of months the tamarins simply vanished. They probably simply went down to the ground and crossed over. Driving, I've seen tamarins cross the

Bearded saki *(Russell A. Mittermeier)*

road just to catch a bug. But the sakis would not do that. They are fruit eaters with a normal range of a couple of hundred hectares; they rapidly hit the relatively few trees in fruit at any given time, taking all the fruit and rarely coming back. But in an isolated ten-hectare patch they didn't have that option, and under pressure they kept returning to the same trees and ate the buds, leaves, and even twigs. Eventually one disappeared and then the other. Either they starved or they finally overcame whatever hesitancy had prevented them from crossing over that sixty or seventy open meters into the forest on the other side."

From such observations, the project's scientists are beginning to make broader generalizations. Lovejoy has suggested the possibility that species will be lost from fragmented forest patches not in an even flow, but in ecologically related clusters. The army ant is an example. As columns of these headstrong creatures march across the forest floor, clouds of fleeing insects form above them. Specialized birds, some known as antbirds, follow the marching ants and feed on the insects they flush. When the ants vanish from a forest patch too small to sustain them, the birds disappear as well. Rankin has written of "significant changes in tree population dynamics" that have already occurred as forest patches in the study areas have become isolated. Other modifications have been documented as well. The edge of an isolated forest patch, Rankin has found, is notably drier, warmer, and windier than the heart of the forest. As a consequence of this change in the microclimate, the number of wind-thrown and upright dead trees at the windward edges tends to increase in a "most striking" manner. Isolation also dramatically lowered the rates of seed survival and seedling establishment of one large tree that was watched with particular intensity. Such are the beginnings of the compendium of information that is expected to emerge from the project. While Lovejoy agrees with Bierregaard that not all the data hoped for can be acquired in a mere twenty years, he remains confident that the job will be done someday. "The point is not *if* one can but *when* one can," he says. "For the shorter term, simply studying the process of species loss is very useful in helping us understand what we are dealing with, and how we might manage smaller areas to retain the largest possible number of species."

Until recent years there was hardly a scientist, let alone an entrepreneur or government official, who felt that "ecosystem decay"—or "ecological dandruff," as Lovejoy has called it—represented a problem for Amazonia. The rubber collapse had put an end to almost every sort of interest in the region, including that of scientists during the 1920s and 1930s. The infrastructure for receiving foreign visitors had fallen into disarray, funds for research expeditions were scarce during the Depression, and the failure of the early development experiments had dampened enthusiasm. In reports published by those few scientists who managed to work in Amazonia between the two world wars, references to the great nineteenth-century explorations seems almost as numerous as those made to more contemporary work. Those who did work the region, such as the researchers brought to Belterra and Fordlândia by the Ford Motor Company, usually came with development rather than conservation as their objective. "Until a short time ago," wrote Vivaldo Cambell de Araújo, then a researcher at INPA, in a paper delivered in 1967, "the idea of creating forest reserves in Amazonia was thought to be absurd. Everyone was always thinking of the inexhaustible riches of our immense forests."

The resource pressures caused by World War II provoked a revival of that stubborn enthusiasm. In Amazonia, there arrived a new generation of young scientists whose mission was to organize the basin's contribution to the war effort. Ironically, members of this group were to make the benchmark observations and discoveries that led toward a new paradigm suggesting that fragility, not fertility, was the region's basic underlying characteristic. One such pioneer was an energetic agronomist named Felisberto de Camargo, who came to Amazonia as chief of the Instituto Agronômico do Norte, the principal Amazonia agricultural development agency of the time. Camargo studied the production of rubber, of jute, of pineapples and other tropical fruits. He found a species of insect that happily ate the rust plaguing some varieties of Amazonian rice. After Henry Ford turned his Amazon plantations over to the Brazilian government at the end of World War II, it became Camargo's responsibility to manage these unrewarding properties. He applied heavy doses of fertilizer to the trees and was struck by the degree to which their yields improved. The experience convinced him, conversely, that the soil itself was not—as observers from Charles de la Condamine to Henry Walter Bates had assumed—the essential factor nurturing the great exuberant Amazonian biomass. To be sure, there had been hints. Spruce's exhaustive findings stimulated further study among the brave little group of mostly British and German scientists who carried on after most interest in Amazonia ended with the rubber crash. Results included many papers by the British botanist P. W. Richards, whose classic 1952 volume, *The Tropical Rain Forest*, contains a full description of the generally acid and nutrient-shy characteristics of its soils. The soil scientist Hans Jenny, of the University of California at Berkeley, also documented the unfavorable chemistry of Amazonian soils in papers published during the mid-1940s. Still, says João Murça Pires, the distinguished senior botanist still working in Belém, "Camargo was the first to cast serious doubt on the fertility of the region."

Camargo and other researchers soon concluded that in thinking about the quality of Amazonian soils, a sharp distinction had to be made between the *várzea* floodplains and the predominant upland, or *terra firme*, over which the annual high waters rarely or never wash. The sediment in most of the *várzea* areas came not from the ancient, weathered Brazilian and Guiana shields but from the far younger Andes, whose volcanic crust contains ample supplies of the mineral nutrients that provide basic support for plant life. Because of steep slopes and strong weathering characteristics in the mountains, these mineral particles wash in ample quantities, suspended in the water, into Amazonia during the flood seasons. When the waters recede, sediments containing these fresh supplies of nutrients are deposited on the shores, already relatively richly endowed from previous flood seasons. Traditional Amazonian agriculture was practiced almost exclusively on the *várzea* lands during the low-water seasons.

The source of the *terra firme* soils turns out to be sharply different. These were derived from the ancient bedrock of the Brazilian and Guianan shields, nutrient-poor to begin with, and further weathered and leached by heavy tropical rains for hundreds of millions of years. In the absence of subsequent geological activity such as new mountain-building in the region, its soils tend to be acid and highly deficient in nutrients. Within the region there is considerable variety. It does little justice to western regions such as Rondônia, a "pre-Andean" zone whose soil is considerably better than that predominating on the central Amazonian upland, to suggest that the only good land is on the *várzea*. However, red and yellow oxisols and ultisols, less fertile than, but similar to, the hardscrabble clays of the U.S. southeast, are far more commonplace on the *terra firme*. And even these soils are more productive than the white sand *campinas*, which represent the extremity of infertility in Amazonia. These bleached sand podzols, similar to the ground underlying the Pine Barrens of New Jersey, occur along rivers such as the Rio Negro and the Tocantins. The only vegetation on them is sparse and scrubby.

If Camargo and his contemporaries concluded correctly that the nutrients were not to be found in the soils, what then of the abundant Amazonian waters? Humboldt had observed that some of these, such as the Solimões, are "white," thanks to the heavy loads of silt they carry. He also referred to "clear" waters such as the Tocantins, and to the "black" or tea-colored waters of the Rio Negro. Once again, almost 150 years elapsed before a significant further scientific analysis of these basic classifications was accomplished. In this instance, the instigator was the German limnologist (student of freshwater ecology) Harald Sioli. By chance on a working visit to Brazil when World War II broke out, Sioli lay low for two years at a remote mission in Amazonia and studied the region at leisure. Interned later in the war with many Brazilian Japanese at a concentration camp near the town of Tomé-Açu in the state of Pará, he observed their increasingly successful efforts to grow black pepper and certain other crops in the region and continued his studies. By the early 1950s, now affiliated with the Max Planck Institute, Sioli was well positioned to begin publishing his findings about the waters of Amazonia.

What he and his colleagues came to understand, in the course of analyses conducted throughout the basin during the 1950s and 1960s, bears a close relationship to what was concurrently being discovered about the soils. The "white" waters flowing down from the Andes, with their heavy loads of suspended minerals, are far and away the richest of the basin. They are no more than slightly acid, and they are capable of supporting a variety of forms of *várzea* life, including foods such as a tropical form of wild rice bearing little resemblance to the North American delicacy bearing the same name. The "white" rivers—the Solimões, the Japurá, the Putumayo, the Napo, the Ucayali, the Madeira—are also far more abundant in aquatic life than other sorts of rivers in Amazonia. The fish eaten in Manaus are almost all caught in the Solimões and the Japurá; the Rio Negro, in contrast, supplies only about 12 percent of the total. The "white" rivers, however, spread their mineral riches over only about 2 percent of the entire basin, and constitute no more than 12 percent of its total drainage. The principal "clear" or transparent waters— the Xingu, the Tapajós—flow not down from the Andes but from the long-leached Tertiary sediments on the shields, and carry very little suspended material. The "black" waters are, by and large, even less capable of supporting life. What causes their distinctive color is tannin from decaying vegetation under the surface, but in other respects they are little different from the "clear" waters. Both clear- and black-water rivers, Sioli and his colleagues found, have properties all but identical to distilled water. That is why we could drink the water of the Uaupés—and why we were lucky to have found good *piraíba* there.

While science was thus defining more clearly the frailty of Amazonia's underpinnings, researchers were concurrently making ever more detailed examinations of the other side of the Amazonian paradox. At the broadest level, they began to look carefully at the extent of the Amazonian biomass (total volume of living matter), which typically weighs in at about five hundred tons per hectare—about twice the weight existing in a typical temperate forest. Even here, some stopped to question what the raw numbers meant, and arrived at the conclusion that leaves and large root systems are the reasons for the excess; the biomass of harvestable tree trunks is about the same as in the temperate forest. Those who have crowed about the higher "productivity" of the tropical forest, then, have erred in thinking that sheer volume indicates great fertility.

Scientists now began also to scrutinize the astonishing diversity of the forest's parts as well as the sheer size of the whole. Although no one knows the final tally, it is supposed that Amazonia contains at least ten percent of all the species, each defined as an organism that is capable of reproducing itself, to be found on the planet. Since estimates of all the world's species range from three to ten million, Amazonia therefore contains somewhere between 300,000 and one million different kinds of living things. Most of the Amazonian species are invertebrates; the variety of larger and more visible forms of life is also impressive. There are perhaps two thousand tree species, tenfold as many as in the temperate forests, and a perplexing total of at least fifty thousand plant varieties; thus Judy Rankin's inability to distinguish between many all but identical species. One thousand species of birds, 2,500 of fish, and an unknown number of invertebrates inhabit Amazonia. Biologically, this region is the most diverse on earth.

Having learned something of the sheer mass and wild profusion of what exists in this forest, though, the scientists also tackled the other obvious question: how an ecosystem with such frail underpinnings could support such abundance. The answers are far from complete. Theories continue to compete for respect among scientists, but some generalizations can safely be made. One very simple factor is the Amazonian climate. In temperate forests, annual frosts kill off a high percentage of herbivorous insects. Since it never freezes in Amazonia, tree species that survive are those that have developed other ways to "escape" from insect predation or disease. Separation—the maximum feasible physical distance between examples of the same species— is thus a characteristic of successful trees in Amazonia. The converse is also important. The farther apart from each other are individuals of any given species, the more opportunity exists for different species to take up the intervening spaces.

If the trees of the Amazonian forest must seek protection from predators, they are also constantly engaged in competition for the precious light that makes photosynthesis possible. In a crowded ecosystem where trees can be fully two hundred feet high, and where not every species can find its way onto the crown of the canopy, many of them have developed special adaptations that enable them to get along with relatively little light or to make rapid use of very short periods of direct sunlight filtering through the canopy. Beginning with P. W. Richards, scientists have frequently asserted the fight for light as a principal cause of the great biological diversity of plant life in Amazonia as in other tropical forest regions. But stating the cause of the diversity is easier than explaining it. In trying, Richards leans toward the zoological notion of the "ecological niche"—the unique amalgam of nutritional and spatial re-quirements that each species occupies, and that permits coexistence with other species sharing some common resources. Neither this concept, known as the "competitive exclusion principle," nor niche theory generally, are usually ap-plied to the trees of the rain forest; within its clutter, so many species so closely resemble each other that the competitive exclusion principle becomes difficult to apply. "How many niches one hundred species occupy," Richards has writ-ten, "must remain one of the 64,000-dollar questions of tropical ecology." Still, he has suggested, the niche theory can "in some modified way" be applied to tropical plants.

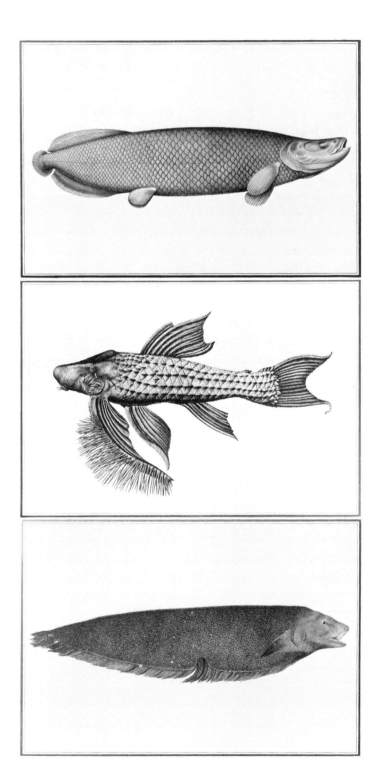

Three fish species as depicted during the Rodrigues Ferreira expedition

What, then, of animals and fishes and other more mobile creatures, as well as the relatively stationary plants? In 1959, Yale's pioneer ecologist, G. Evelyn Hutchinson, posed the question with disarming simplicity. "Why," he asked, "are there so many kinds of animals?" As answers, scientists pose a quagmire of differing theories beginning with the relatively simple zoological idea of the ecological niche. How, over time, these niches were established, and how speciation occurred, are thought to have to do with geological change over the eras, and with the notion that temporary physical barriers brought about biological diversification. The view generally accepted during the early twentieth century was that most speciation in Amazonia took place during the relatively early Tertiary period, as a result of barriers imposed by the great Andean upheaval, and that there were no major changes later on. In 1969, however, a German ornithologist and paleoclimatologist named Jurgen Haffer, who at the time was working for Mobil in Dallas, suggested that the far more recent Pleistocene climate changes had much to do with the process, at least insofar as a certain number of bird species are concerned. According to the so-called "refuge theory" that he proposed in a benchmark article published that year in *Science* magazine, the basin was fragmented during the several dry climatic periods that occurred during the Pleistocene. There developed

a number of smaller forests which were isolated from each other by tracts of open, nonforest vegetation. The remaining forests served as "refuge areas" for numerous populations of forest animals, which deviated from one another during periods of geographic isolation. The isolated forests were again united during humid climatic periods when the intervening open country became once more forest-covered, permitting the refuge-area populations to extend their ranges. This rupturing and rejoining of the various forests in Amazonia probably was repeated several times during the Quaternary that followed the Tertiary, and led to a rapid differentiation of the Amazonian forest fauna in geologically very recent times.

The Brazilian zoologist P. E. Vanzolini has corroborated Haffer's general findings with his studies of certain lizards. Plant data compiled by Ghillean T. Prance of the New York Botanical Garden, a veteran of almost twenty years of Amazonian study who in many senses has continued work that Spruce began 150 years ago, has provided further confirmation.

The details of Haffer's refuge theory are, nevertheless, still hotly debated. Recently, an entire scientific conference was held on the subject, and what was most generally felt was that no one theory can explain all tropical speciation. "Where the refuge theory doesn't work, population biology interpretations do," wrote an ant specialist, Woodruff W. Benson of the University of Campinas in southern Brazil, referring to the idea that when a niche fills up, new adaptations tend to occur. So much general ignorance of the process remains, wrote John R. G. Turner of the University of Leeds in England, "that we are in no position to reject any plausible model *a priori.*" That the Pleistocene refuges played a role is now, however, not widely contested. The eminent Smithsonian Institution anthropologist Betty J. Meggers, a keen student of Amazonia for four decades, has called it "the first satisfactory solution to the enigma."

The never-ending search for biological success in the crowded and busy Amazonian ecosystem, scientists continue to find, involves a number of truly remarkable relationships between individual species. Worked out over the millennia, their special forms often enable both species partners to survive. The relationship between food and seed dispersal—essential if tree species are to avoid extinction through predation—has been frequently noted. Bates was among the early visitors to observe the phenomenon of ravenous fishes gathering under fruit trees and churning the waters as eagerly as bluefish after sardines, as fruits from the flooded forest fell to the surface of the water. In recent years several scientists, particularly a determined Californian named Michael Goulding, have reached close understanding of how the phenomenon works—especially in nutrient-shy rivers such as the Negro. Many of the fish have adapted to eat only in the flood season, when fruit is available, and to survive on accumulated fats for the remainder of the year. The fruit trees, in turn, are dependent on the fish to disperse the seeds, widely enough to provide insurance against disease and predation, after having eaten the fruit surrounding them. Also, the agouti, a rabbit-sized rodent that ranges relatively widely in search of nuts, buries more of them than it can later locate. It too performs the double task of dispersing and planting seeds from the forest. Birds, bats, and monkeys are other species that carry out similar missions.

Pollination is often accomplished in elaborate ways that protect flowers from predation by insects that consume only nectar. *Bertholletia excelsa,* the principal species of the tree that produces the protein-rich Brazil nut, is an example. Its flower has a particularly strong outer petal that lies flat across the end of the blossom. To crawl into the center of the flower and reach its nectar, and also be dusted by pollen, the pollinator must have sufficient strength to shoulder past the formidable outer barrier. Only one species of Amazonian bee is up to the job, and the tree is therefore dependent upon it. The bee, on the other hand, can survive only in a forest of sufficient diversity to sustain it when *Bertholletia excelsa* is not in flower. Another example is provided by the flowers of bat-pollinated plants, which usually point toward the ground to enable bats to eat comfortably as they hang head-down. Although most are yet to be observed, tropical biologists assume the existence of myriad other examples of special symbiotic ways in which Amazonian plants, animals, and insects reinforce each other. They view our poor understanding of these intricate polli-

The agouti (top) and an example of one of the myriad frog species in Amazonia. To be important in the ecosystem, an individual species need not be itself of great importance. (Above: *Russell A. Mittermeier;* below: *Roger D. Stone*)

nation relationships as a principal example of how much remains to be learned about Amazonia.

No process in the Amazonian ecosystem is more complex or more fascinating than the means by which its scarce nutrients (potassium, calcium, magnesium) are captured and recycled. In the temperate forest, the rich layer of topsoil serves as a storehouse for nutrients, and large trees typically possess a fairly deep, if not extensive, root system serving in part as a means of absorbing them. Amazonian plant life, however, cannot subsist on the scant nutrient supplies to be found in the acid and barren ground upon which the trees are precariously anchored. A team of ecologists headed by Dr. Carl F. Jordan of the University of Georgia has, after many years of studying plant life around the Venezuelan town of San Carlos on the upper Rio Negro, come to a detailed understanding of how they get along under these circumstances. Successful trees have, for one thing, developed dense mats of fine, shallow roots that do not tap into the ground, but rather "attack" the thin (one- to three-centimeter) layer of leaf litter falling twelve months a year to the forest floor. "When leaves, fruit, or branches fall," Jordan has written, "the roots soon cover and attach to the decomposing litter. A few months later, all that is left is a shell of roots, showing the shape of the decomposed litter."

During their studies, Jordan and his multinational colleagues (who have included Hans Klinge from Germany's Max Planck Institute, Rafael Herrera

An Amazonian tree in search of nutrients *(Richard O. Bierregaard)*

from the Venezuelan Institute for Scientific Investigations, and Christopher Uhl of Penn State University) have closely analyzed many other ways in which Amazonian trees manage to survive on slender nutrient budgets. For one thing, they shed and replace their leaves at a relatively constant rate throughout the year, thus avoiding the need for the energy-consuming leafing-out effort that temperate deciduous trees make each spring even though the *total* number of leaves produced may be greater. The *hyphae* or threads of fungi, Herrera has found, act as ducts through which certain kinds of nutrients pass from litter to living root. The forest even scavenges some nutrients contained in rainfall before the water hits the ground, by means of roots that grow *up* the tree trunks. Certain species of mosses, algae, and lichens, Uhl and Jordan have both reported, can capture nutrients from rainfall and fix nitrogen from air. At INPA, the hydrologist Wolfram Franken is studying in detail the near-complete extent to which the forest absorbs nutrients from rainfall. Using sensitive instruments, he has established that whereas rain entering his study area contains one hundred grams of phosphorus per hectare, no more than three grams per hectare are allowed out. Various mechanisms, then, enable the forest to retain its nutrients in a series of virtually closed loops between the sky, the trees, and the earth surface; only a tiny fraction escapes the cycles and leaches into the subsoil.

Klinge and Sioli have jointly done much to describe the broad significance of the relationship between rivers, rainfall, and rain forest in Amazonia. Evapotranspiration, the process by which moisture returns from the earth's surface back into the atmosphere, originates not only in the rivers and on the ground but in the trees themselves, which collect and store ample quantities of moisture. Clouds form and the water falls back to earth in form of rain showers or, frequently, severe storms. The leaves of the trees "catch" rainfall and the water gently rolls off their typical "drip tips" onto the ground beneath, thus avoiding erosion. Then the dense root system, which according to Klinge is three times the size of the temperate forest's, reclaims the water and it is recirculated within the trees. Even during the dry season, Sioli has stated, the trees themselves supply much of the humidity that the forest requires.

Eneas Salati, a former INPA director who now works at the University of São Paulo, has long been studying the movement of air and moisture across the basin. Half or less of the rainwater that falls on Amazonia, he has found, enters the basin in the form of clouds formed over the Atlantic and then blown westward by prevailing winds. The remaining portion comes from within the basin, largely in the form of transpiration from the forest, and is the principal factor maintaining the stability of the regional climate. The removal of the forest, Salati and many other scientists fear, would result in a regional drying trend leading toward perhaps even the desertification of what is still now perpetually moist forest. The forest, as we shall see in Chapter 9, plays other

Shortly before an afternoon squall on the Uaupés *(Roger D. Stone)*

formidable roles: as a vast storehouse for carbon that would otherwise be released into the atmosphere, and as a guardian against erosion and flooding. "The dynamic equilibrium of the Amazonian ecosystem depends on the forest," Salati concludes.

"In its undisturbed state, the Amazonian forest is just as robust as any other forest," says Jordan. It is only when it is cut, he continues, that leaching, erosion, species loss, and other forms of instability make it "fragile." Through the efforts of the contemporary field scientists cited here, and many others, the extent and consequences of this vulnerability are being more clearly, more precisely defined than ever before. At the same time, the diversity within the forest is also being put into sharper focus. In sum, however, what science has generally established over the past thirty years, about the forest's fascinating delicate complexity, should make even the boldest dreamer a skeptic about the prospects for developing Amazonia.

CHAPTER 7

The New and Ancient Ways

ONE HUNDRED YEARS AGO, WORKERS BEGAN TO RAZE THE VIRGIN FOREST from Belém, at the mouth of the Amazon, to the town of Bragança, three hundred kilometers to the east. They built a railroad that was completed in 1908. Into the newly accessible territories poured government-sponsored colonists from Spain and Portugal, France and the Azores. Others arrived spontaneously from the drought-scoured and always dirt-poor cow country of the Brazilian northeast. The colonists clear-cut the forest and planted beans and rice, corn and manioc. For a few years all went well. But then the crops began to fail and all but a few of the colonists drifted away. When the rubber era ended, the railroad, which never turned a cruzeiro's worth of profit, shut down as well. Soon the so-called Zona Bragantina had not only been shorn of thirty thousand square kilometers of prime forest, but was all but abandoned as well. Once envisioned as the Arcadia of the neotropics, the Bragantina had by the 1950s become what the pioneer scientist Eugênia Egler memorably called a "ghost landscape."

Several years ago, curious to see what had more recently happened in this infamous part of Amazonia, I set forth from Belém along the well-paved

What is left of the railroad into the Zona Bragantina is
this train-statue. *(Roger D. Stone)*

highway to Bragança that long ago replaced the railroad. David Oren, an
ecologist and ornithologist who works at the Museu Emílio Goeldi in Belém
("The City of the Mango Trees"), accompanied me. As we drove westward across the flatlands, we saw little evidence of productive human activity.
Subsistence-level plantings at the roadside alternated with patches of the
second-growth forest known locally as *capoeira* and consisting largely of woody
species such as cecropia that make an easy adaptation to the high-light conditions that prevail after the forest is felled. Pastures were weedy and few cattle
could be seen. Near one town, smoke spewed from the smokestack of a shabby
old cement plant totally unequipped with pollution controls. The fallout had
turned everything visible a dusty, choking brown.

Oren, who won his doctorate at Harvard and then obtained a permanent
visa to live and work in Brazil and a position as assistant researcher at the
museum, displayed sharp-tongued dismay at the biological wreckage we were
witnessing. Just as the ants and antbirds had gone from Rob Bierregaard's
forest fragments near Manaus, so had the deforestation of the Bragantina
triggered drastic species attrition. With the loss of habitat for the brightly

colored birds of the *cotinga* family, the avocadolike trees whose fruits the birds ate and whose seed they dispersed quickly vanished as well. Small rodents are virtually the only mammals left on land that once provided cover for jaguars, tapirs, peccaries, and many monkeys. "Luxuriant high forest was transformed into extensive stretches of stunted scrub," Sioli had written of the Bragantina, "and only a few skeletons, now becoming rarer and rarer, of isolated trees still testify to the former exuberant growth in the region."

Is the Bragantina destined to remain as degraded as it appears? Or might chemicals, bulldozers, and the other tools of contemporary technology bring about a more positive outcome in the future? In search of clues, I turned to Ítalo Cláudio Falesi, an energetic and seasoned agronomist who was then serving as the ranking agricultural development official in the state of Pará. Unhesitatingly, Falesi agreed that the Bragantina had indeed fallen to the nadir that Sioli and Oren lamented, but, he added, that had been perhaps twenty years ago, and a remarkable transformation had since taken place. Falesi arranged a second sortie for me, in order to see the change, little of which was visible from the highway. This time I would ride with Eduardo Ohashi, an agronomist from Falesi's department. Again we drove from Belém eastward, toward Bragança. Most of the farmers we visited were post–World War II emigrants from Japan, who had joined the small Japanese-Brazilian colony that had been founded in Tomé-Açu, Pará, in the 1920s. The initial efforts to develop cocoa plantations there had failed, and malaria had felled many of the settlers. Further farming experiments there were interrupted by World War II, during which the Japanese at Tomé-Açu were confined in the concentration camp in which Sioli, too, spent part of the war. But in 1945, with the end of the war, many of the former inmates stayed in Tomé-Açu, growing principally the Singapore variety of black pepper plant whose spicy fruit had become a staple export crop for Brazil. Then, in the 1960s, when a disease began to beset the black pepper monocultures that the Japanese had developed in the Tomé-Açu region, many pulled up stakes and reoccupied the Bragantina.

Here, on land that had never been sustainably productive since the deforestation of several decades before, these Japanese agribusinessmen were now using fertilizers, pesticides, heavy machines—even underground irrigation systems of the kind installed in California's lush Imperial Valley—to grow commercial crops on fields discreetly hidden behind the stands of *capoeira* facing the highways. One prominent farmer, the president of the producers' cooperative in a bustling town called Castanhal, which lies in the heart of the Bragantina, was employing three hundred workers and grossing the equivalent of $80,000 a month by raising the juicy burnt-orange papayas of Pará that are known as the best in Brazil, and trucking them 3,200 kilometers to the wholesale market in São Paulo. The cooperative was also considering a $500,000 investment in a plant to process the fruit of the Dendé or African oil palm,

Modern agriculture in the Zona Bragantina. Growing papayas can be profitable for the few Amazonians who can afford to buy the insecticide and spray the crop. *(Roger D. Stone)*

an import said to do well in the region. Another farmer was experimenting with a hybrid strain of black pepper plant that had been developed by the federal government's agricultural research department and would, if successful, yield fifty percent more than the traditional variety. Cocoa, melons, and other fruits were also being commercially grown by the Bragantina's new entrepreneurs. According to Ohashi, the future beckons. With proper seeds and fertilizers, he explained, crop yields in the region could rise by as much as 1,000 percent. I asked if the region could become as productive for agriculture as even the most fertile lands of California or France. "Oh yes," said Ohashi with a soft smile. "I think so."

Between agronomists such as Ohashi or Falesi and the apprehensive environmentalists, there is no disagreement about what happens during the typical Amazonian cycle of clear-cutting and burning to make way for farms. After they have been cut by chainsaws or pushed over by bulldozers, the large trees of the original forest are allowed to dry for several months. Then the fallen biomass is set afire. Parasites, fungi, insects, nematodes, and pathogenic bacteria are killed. Artificially sanitary conditions for agriculture are created. The ashes formed by the fires, moreover, contain rich stores of the mineral nutrients that had been locked into the deadly efficient recycling system of the original forest. Decomposing tree trunks, which tend not to be fully burned, also enrich the soil. For several years of cultivation it is fertile enough to support most basic crops such as rice, corn, or manioc. Then, however, the nutrients are lost through leaching. The soil reverts to its previous acid, barren, sometimes toxic condition. Crop yields lower to the point where traditional practitioners of shifting or slash-and-burn agriculture—the classic farming system of the humid tropics—simply move on to new forest to repeat the cycle. At this point a farmer tied to a set tract of land is out of luck, at least for the short term, unless he can afford expensive fertilizers.

If grasses are planted on the cleared land in preparation for the introduction of cattle, a similar pattern occurs. For the first few years, even *Panicum maximum* or *"colonião,"* the ordinary grass of the region, grows profusely, thanks to the ample "flush" of nutrients available. Other grass varieties that consume fewer nutrients survive longer. No matter what sort of grass is planted, however, the predictable downward spiral begins at some point unless expensive fertilizer is applied. Critical nutrients—especially phosphorus and potassium— become increasingly scarce because the intricate ecosystem that had supplied them no longer exists. Weeds, able to get along on tighter nutrient budgets than the pasture grasses, or to grow faster in the bright sunlight, begin to reoccupy the land. Some species are toxic and themselves kill cattle. Others simply replace the grass and crowd it out. Compaction, resulting from trampling as well as from the loss of the forest canopy, causes the soil to be increasingly subject to leaching and erosion. (In some areas there even occurs a process called laterization, in which the ground turns almost as hard as

A major threat: cattle grazing on recently deforested land *(Roger D. Stone)*

concrete.) Within a few years of the burn, the amount of land required to support a single head of cattle increases from an initial one hectare to a typical four or five hectares, or even—according to the botanist Joao Murça Pires—an astonishing thirteen to fifteen hectares in some particularly unpromising corners of Amazonia. "Much of the area converted to pasture," wrote the UCLA ecologist Susanna B. Hecht in a delicious understatement, "is only ephemerally productive."

To those attempting large-scale plantation agriculture in Amazonia, the nutrient-loss problem is but one of several limiting factors. "Perhaps more important," said the University of Georgia's Carl Jordan, "are insects, fungi, and other predators and parasites which can take advantage of the unique conditions of monocultures, i.e., the unlimited, genetically undifferentiated resource coupled with a hot, wet climate unbroken by dry or cold seasons which could interrupt the predators' exponential growth." In the natural forest, Jordan explains, plants that are "host species" for predatory insects occur only sporadically. The insects have to travel long distances to get from one host to the next. En route, birds and other insect eaters reduce the predator populations. In plantations, however, the host species are massed together and provide tempting targets for insect invasions. At the same time, many of their natural enemies have lost their habitats. Bierregaard's studies, for instance, provide dramatic proof of what happens to bird populations during the deforestation that precedes the installation of the plantations. The leaf blight that defeated Henry Ford is caused by a fungus called *Microcyclus ulei* that is controllable in places where a pronounced dry season occurs—but devastating even at Ford-lândia and Belterra, which are some of the driest places anywhere in Amazonia.

If there is little disagreement about these sort of patterns, what to make of them is still keenly debated in the scientific community. Many see the problems of soils and insects as nothing more than further surmountable obstacles along the path to Amazonian "conquest." Among U.S. Amazonists, a voluble spokesman for the viability of agricultural development in the basin is Pedro A. Sanchez, soil science professor at North Carolina State University, whose work is supported by the Agency for International Development. In a number of papers based on his field experience at Yurimaguas in Peru, at the very western end of the basin, Sanchez has stressed the issue's positive aspects. He admits that only about six percent of Amazonia, or 31 million hectares, is composed of soils "with no major limitations" that can support important commercial crops such as cocoa. But, he continues, the weaknesses of the soils that predominate in Amazonia are chemical rather than physical, and therefore subject to correction. Amazonian soils tend to drain well, and erosion has been caused more by sloppy civic engineering than by farming. Overall, he believes, continuous cropping of acid and infertile Amazonian soils is quite possible if "intensively managed rotation systems" are employed (monocultures carry too much risk of disease). Applying what Sanchez calls "adequate fertilization," farmers he has monitored have successfully grown corn, rice, soybeans, and peanuts in "continuous production" at Yurimaguas.

In an article published in *Science* in May 1982, Sanchez and several co-authors cited six- to tenfold increases in yields there after the introduction of the "Yurimaguas method," and alleged that average family incomes had risen four-fold—from $750 to $3,000 for each 1.5 hectares in cultivation. To be sure, they warned, the experience could not be replicated everywhere. There must be good access to markets, and adequate technological capabilities must be available; weed, pest, and disease problems may be more severe elsewhere than at Yurimaguas. (Though they firmly denied that the soil was better than average, the location of Sanchez's study area at the western end of the basin, close to the Andes, was enough to suggest relatively favorable conditions.) Their broad conclusion, though, was that agriculture in Amazonia was generally capable of becoming as sophisticated as that practiced in the southeastern United States, "where shifting cultivation was the predominant system only a few decades ago." They even claimed that the system they advocated would "have a positive ecological impact," in that "for every hectare that is cleared and put into such production, many hectares of forest may be spared from the shifting cultivator's ax in his search to grow the same amount of food." Paulo de Tarso Alvim, research director of the Brazilian institute that studies cocoa-growing techniques and a prominent spokesman for Amazonian development, puts it in terms of human well-being: "Shifting agriculture always will continue to be a subsistence system, incapable of improving appreciably the level of living of the farmer. Agricultural research can contribute to perfecting self-sustaining systems so that they raise the level of commercial exploitation."

For successful cattle ranching on Amazonian *terra firme*, Falesi prescribes a combination of weed control, fertilizer application, and adequate rest periods. Although the principal government agencies involved no longer believe in the efficacy of deforestation to make way for cattle ranches, they still advocate remedies for already degraded pastures, of which there are at least 800,000 hectares in Amazonia, and perhaps also for an additional 3.3 million hectares that are classified as "threatened." On such lands Falesi has suggested complete replanting with such special grass as an African variety called *Brachiaria humidicola* that tolerates both acid soil and a troublesome pest called the spittlebug. Despite the considerable evidence to the contrary, Falesi concluded in a recent paper that Amazonia "can be considered to have a great animal protein production potential, using the cultivation pastures as raw material, if the pasture is established and managed as a true crop."

To Falesi and Alvim and others with Panglossian tinges to their views of development prospects in Amazonia, no grand scheme heralded greater promise than D. K. Ludwig's Jari. The initial results obtained there, Alvim wrote in a paper published in 1978, bespoke the "enormous potential for commercial silviculture in the Amazon." Even when things went wrong, the blame was placed on poor management or lack of continuity or Ludwig's dictatorial methods rather than on any fundamental lack of soundness in the grand design. "The problems were ones of planning and not of biology," said Charles Briscoe, the former head of Jari's Division of Forest Management, at a recent symposium on Amazonia. "I still think that the potential there was substantial. But we'll never know."

Judy Rankin and Philip Fearnside, another seasoned ecologist at INPA in Manaus, have arrived at a sharply different judgment. After making three extensive visits to the area, they have become highly skeptical about the sustainability of the project and have urged "extreme caution" about its use as a model. As early as 1978 they detected incipient defects in Jari's silviculture, timber, and pulp operations. The growth rate of the "miracle" *gmelina* trees imported from Asia had been slowed because of sandy soils on most of the 60,000 hectares where they had been planted. Although serious attrition had not occurred, a wide variety of insects had attacked the *gmelina* plantations. The Caribbean pine, a second pulpwood species that Ludwig introduced in 1973—in part because it was so toxic that it was immune to most forms of predation—had been attacked by leaf-cutter ants. Plantings of *Eucalyptus deglupta* had just been undertaken. No fertilizer was being used to accelerate the *gmelina* growth rates, and only guesses could be made about what amounts and costs might eventually be required. Fuel to run the pulp mill was coming from the native forest, which was being consumed at the rate of four hectares per day to keep the machinery turning over. By 1981, when Fearnside and Rankin returned to Jari, officials there had admitted to a "slight decrease" in the *gmelina* growth rates. In order to keep the pulp mill fed, Caribbean pine originally destined to be used as timber was instead being prematurely cut for pulpwood, fifteen percent of which was coming directly from the native forest. Plantation yields, according to Fearnside and Rankin, had sunk to about half of the original estimates. The future hardly looked promising: "Continued removal of nutrients from the system in the form of harvested biomass will eventually deplete stocks of available nutrients to the point where growth is reduced to uneconomic levels." Jordan, too, sees shortcomings in the Jari forestry scheme. "People like Falesi say that conversion of the forest enriches the soil. I say that it enriches the soil, all right, but the whole ecosystem drops way down because of the loss of the nutrients that had been stored in the original biomass. And you use most of what's left just to grow your first crop of pine."

Rice operations on the fertile *várzea* floodplain at São Raimundo, on the Jari property, had gotten off to a spectacular start. Using heavy equipment for land-clearing, and low-flying aircraft for sowing and spraying, Jari technicians had by 1978 planted 3,283 hectares of an envisioned total of 14,165 hectares. The variety used was the long-grained IR-22, one of the "miracle" strains developed primarily for Asia by the New York–based IRI Research Institute. The plan was to export most of Jari's rice and to sell it at world-market prices. An intensive schedule of three harvests per year was resulting in yields that at one point achieved a world record of more than nine tons per hectare. But by the time of Fearnside and Rankin's second visit, "setbacks" had been encountered. These included "iron toxicity, evinced by accumulation of brown sludge on the rice roots"; infestations of army worms, stinkbugs, nematodes, aphids, and mites; diseases including rice blast, leaf scald, and brown leaf spot; and the arrival of several weed species. Yields had lowered and a search for more resistant rice varieties (which tend to be short-grained rather than long-grained and therefore less marketable) was under way. Biological problems could be expected to "become more severe," said the two ecologists, "as additional weeds, pests, and diseases arrive in this new rice-producing area." Economic headaches had cropped up as well: after one crop had been exported, the government required Jari to sell all of its rice on the domestic market at a far lower price. The scientists readily admitted that many of the problems in the Jari rice plantations might be overcome through increasing knowledge, good management, and the sheer application of financial resources; yet they found the overall prospects for the rice project not "encouraging."

Over the past several years, the Jari management has become more tolerant of visits by journalists and environmentalists. Fearnside and Rankin returned for their third survey; Carl Jordan completed the first assessment of the effects of tree rotations on Jari's nutrient budget. Not surprisingly, the findings continue to be negative. The broad point, though, is not whether these scientists are right or wrong in their assessment of the project's future, and not whether it caused great irreparable ecological harm. (It didn't.) The real message of the most ostentatiously broken dream of Amazonia since the collapse of Henry Ford's Belterra lies in the fact that Jari was always insulated from many of the usual problems that most Amazonian farmers face. Capital was available in ample quantities. Since the area was totally under the project managers' control, they could deal with such problems as squatters without legal or political interference. They had full access to the world's knowledge and technology. After fourteen years of existence under such favorable circumstances, Jari was *still* not economic, even under the project's elastic definition of that term. Better managers than Ludwig may succeed with more rationally designed and executed schemes, but almost all will be working with far fewer initial advantages.

Even if a stray Amazonian agriculture project is feasible, as in the instance of the Yurimaguas experiment, it is not necessarily worth the effort. "Sanchez openly admits that a high input of fertilizer is essential there," Jordan says. "Where his argument is really weak is in the area of economic justification for hauling in all that fertilizer all the way across the Andes from Lima. Why not just haul in the food?" From his home base in Athens, Georgia, amid the red-clay soils of the U.S. southeast, Jordan also challenges Sanchez's assertion that Amazonia should aspire to replicate the Georgia model: "Even with the roads and the knowledge and the technology we have," he says, "it's marginal to produce crops and pulpwood in Georgia. How can we expect there to be economic production in a place like Amazonia?" There is only so much room in the domestic and international market for specialized crops, the ones that fetch high market prices, that the Japanese farmers of the Bragantina are successfully producing. "You can pasture on the moon," says Jordan. "All you need to do is send up the nutrients and the water. But what's the point?" Alvim himself suggests that no more than one percent of Amazonia is right for the introduction of perennial or semiperennial crops such as sugar cane or pineapple. What is basically at stake was well stated in a recent essay by the ecologist Susanna Hecht. "The issues surrounding Amazonian deforestation," she wrote, "involve not just the proverbial developer versus environmental tradeoff, but questions about whether the nature of the development path itself is appropriate."

The botanist João Murça Pires puts the matter succinctly. From the needless tragedy of the Bragantina to the failures of the mid-1970s cattle projects and Ludwig's Jari, he has observed the consequences of misinformed "development" efforts. Not a flashy figure himself, he is more often to be found crashing about the back roads in his ancient vehicle (known as "the Yellow Submarine" and redolent of the many samples that have occupied its rear seat) than lobbying in Brasília or Belém. He has not even published many articles. But the knowledge in his head is encyclopedic, and he views what is happening in Amazonia with a wistful sadness and irony. Repeatedly, over the decades, he has watched the cycle that begins with the forest's "opening" for entry by motor vehicle or train, and ends with its death. He is mindful, as are many other Amazon scientists, that the *cerrado*, or savanna lands, bordering Amazonia are far better bets for agriculture or ranching than the lowland forest itself. "Why," he asks plaintively, "can we not have a policy of nondevelopment?"

Most everyone is realistic, though, about the improbability of achieving a complete victory and bringing about a complete halt to Amazonian development. As an alternative, the environmentalists have thought long and hard about the sorts of activities that are both income-producing and sustainable in demanding Amazonia. Hecht, for one, has written convincingly about the dim prospects for Amazonian cattle ranching and plantation agriculture. She professes little enthusiasm for the usual sorts of forestry and timber operations in Amazonia, which have traditionally been carried out by small-scale human predators in response to growing world demand—and high prices—for tropical sawn woods. She does not rule out certain uses of the region's timber resources, recommending the adoption of various sustainable land-management techniques known to scientists as "agroforestry." The term "covers an enormous range of land uses at all scales of tenure and investment," as she has written, but it always involves the occupation of the same space by trees and other plants and sometimes animals as well.

In one agroforestry system, food crops requiring shade or protection from heavy rainfall, such as the bush that produces cocoa, are planted on cleared land; then timber species are introduced. One of the more interesting experiments at Jari was the "silvo-pastoral" system, in which Caribbean pine plantations were seeded with *colonião* grass as ground cover and cattle were introduced. Although the presence of the livestock slowed the trees' growth rate slightly, the compensating advantages were substantial: weed-control problems were eliminated, and some fifty kilos of meat per hectare were produced. If well planned, agroforests tend to be easy to manage, inhibit erosion and pest predation, and encourage high rates of nutrient storage.

There may be room in agroforests for some indigenous plant species that are particularly useful or tasty to *Homo sapiens*. The African oil palm withstands acid soil and aluminum toxicity, a problem often encountered in Amazonia, and its yield can be far greater than that of other oil-producing plants such as the soybean, the peanut, or the olive tree. Many other palm species produce edible fruits as well as cooking or salad oil and thatch for houses. The palm heart, an export crop of growing commercial importance, comes from the common and graceful *açaí* that we encountered along the Uaupés. And the all-purpose *pupunha*, again a palm, does just about everything. The *cupuaçu*, a whitish fruit with a delicious sweet-sour taste and endless aficionados, is only one of almost two hundred edible Amazonian fruits of which no commercial use is now made. Those who care most about the welfare of the region wonder why greater efforts are not made to make fuller use of these sorts of species rather than stamp out their habitats. Hecht and many other scientists place a high priority on doing further studies of sustainable uses for these still largely unknown natural products of the forest.

Beginning with Felisberto Camargo, who considered management techniques to make them more productive, no one has disputed the great potential of the rich *várzeas* for the cultivation of rice and seasonal vegetables. But the floodplains are important also as breeding grounds for Goulding's fruit-eating fish and for other aquatic resources; Betty Meggers is only one of many scientists concerned that overadjustment of natural conditions along the *várzeas* might adversely affect these habitats. Sioli thought that Herman Kahn's au-

Igapô (flooded forest) along the Rio Negro *(Roger D. Stone)*

dacious proposal to dam the lower Amazon and flood several hundred thousand hectares would have "a lasting and permanent effect" on the *várzea*—its disappearance.

Ethnobotanists, pharmaceutical companies, and purveyors of "fragrances" find commercial potential in a host of wild plants to be found in Amazonia's existing forest. For centuries Indian shamans have been using folk-medicine techniques to cure sick people. Now, increasingly, the modern world is finding out that the cures work, and the rush is on to learn what the shamans know before they die and their cultures disappear. Richard E. Schultes and Mark Plotkin, of Harvard University and the Harvard Botanical Museum, have already described a variety of effective herbal medicines. Working deep in the forests of Brazil and Suriname, they have identified various anticancer compounds and contraceptives. "We've barely scratched the surface," says Plotkin, and he adds that many of the substances already known cannot be created synthetically and must come from the wild. Such is the potential in this sector that no more than limited deforestation may in fact be an enormous economic sacrifice, particularly since many yet-unstudied species occur only in small, vulnerable areas.

The prudent use of Amazonia's aquatic resources is also required. During the past twenty years, as the region's population has risen, uncontrolled harvests of food fish have reduced many species dangerously, and turned many of the

An Indian priest, or shaman, shows a curative plant.
(Mark J. Plotkin)

basin's fisheries into aquatic equivalents of the Zona Bragantina. Gill nets, not to speak of the dynamite that is used by fishermen functioning with no concern for legal constraints, severely threaten populations of species upon which Amazonians have relied for protein. Manatees and caimans—both creatures with potentially productive roles in a balanced and carefully managed Amazonian ecosystem—have been driven to the brink of extinction. In the meantime, various sustainable forms of commercially scaled aquaculture have been tested and seem viable. The icthyologist Nigel Smith has stated that a small lake containing a managed population of a river turtle of the genus *Podocnemis* could produce 440 times as much meat as an equivalent amount of Amazonian cattle pasture. Michael Goulding advocates various ways of managing the *várzeas* so that fruit-eating fish can feed for longer portions of the year and thus grow faster. The water buffalo, which produces great and useful quantities of milk, cheese, and meat, thrives in a watery environment and is far less harmful to Amazonia than is the cow. It ranges far less widely and tramples proportionally less vegetation, and its manure fertilizes new crops of the grasses it eats.

There are, then, a number of compelling reasons to think that an appropriate

"development path" for the *terra firme* of Amazonia demands a light touch
rather than a heavy hand. The vulnerable forest has an economic potential that
might be greater for the long term if used largely in its natural state. Realistically, then, is the ideal future for Amazonia one of low population density
and limited use? Is there no viable use for this region, once thought to hold
such great economic promise, other than to provide sustenance for a few
million *caboclos* and a better living for a few clever entrepreneurs such as the
Japanese of the Bragantina? Not entirely, for the big new entrant in the Amazonian development sweepstakes is mining. The scope and magnitude of the
mineral-development schemes that have been launched in the past decade cause
even Jari to pale into insignificance. Mining has, on the one hand, greatly
inflated the estimates of Amazonia's economic potential—and has, at the same
time, heightened concern about environmental consequences.

   One might well ponder upon the finite nature of mining as an activity. No
matter how huge the deposits of minerals, they eventually run out. At that
point the local citizenry, be it in Alaska or in California or in Carajás, is once
again forced to think about what happens next. Generically, then, mining is
no more of a permanent solution for Amazonia than were Orellana's search
for cinnamon trees, or the colonists' interest in the *drogas do sertão*, or the
rubber era. But the minerals boom has put Amazonia on its most dramatic
roll in a century—and the phenomenon is worth a detailed investigation.

CHAPTER 8

Crossing the Line

THE HISTORY OF MARANHÃO HAS FEW MOMENTS OF GREATNESS. THERE was the time of the occupation by the French, early in the seventeenth century, and their subsequent replacement by a Portuguese force. During the era of slavery, it was economical to grow cotton on Maranhão's savanna lands. The pretty colonial island town of São Luís, on the Atlantic Ocean, served as the port of departure for the annual crops. But the end of slavery by and large rendered the cotton industry uneconomical, and both Maranhão and São Luís reverted to a state of torpor that persisted well into this century. In 1966 I first went there, and here, in part, is what I wrote:

Last year Maranhão, to the east of the state of Pará and on the eastern fringe of Amazonia, distinguished itself by having become Brazil's poorest state. It exists in purgatory, half in the poor arid northeast to the south and east, half in Amazonia to the west. It has little trade with the outside world and virtually no local industry. Seventy-six percent of the 3.5 million people are illiterate and the population grows 5.5 percent a year, thanks to internal birth rates and immigration from other northeastern states. It has only seven kilometers of paved highway, 10,000 kilowatts of electric power, one doctor per 250,000 people outside the capital city of São Luís. Almost everybody in the state has worms of some kind; one of every four has had malaria. Life expectancy is somewhere between twenty-nine and thirty-two years (state statisticians cannot agree on a firm figure). As a grim reminder of 350-year-old São Luís's past, there are slave quarters in the basement of the downtown building where the Booth shipping line now does business. Buzzards feast on the smelly streets of São Luís. Pigs, chickens, and swollen-bellied children grub in the garbage. Medical attention is something dreadful. Just a year ago in São Luís, the then government abandoned the two hundred patients of a state tuberculosis hospital. The sole doctor and the hospital director were dismissed, the kitchen and the laundry were closed, meals were restricted to one ration of bread and water a day. The smells in the toilets, the filth of the sleeping quarters were unimaginable.

A while ago, with the charnel-house atmosphere surrounding that previous visit still crisp in my brain, I returned to São Luís to see what changes had been wrought there. Close to twenty years of military government have perhaps brought about some improvements. Prosperity must have accompanied the focal role of São Luís in the Grande Carajás scheme; two port facilities were being built there. One was for the Companhia Vale do Rio Doce to use to export its Carajás iron ore; the other was for Alumar, the Maranhão Aluminum Consortium, whose principal shareholder is Alcoa. In addition to its port, the Alumar project includes the construction of a $1.5-billion smelting and refining complex that will eventually be able to produce two million tons of alumina (the substance extracted from bauxite from which aluminum is made) a year. Some of this alumina will be exported; some will be used to help the plant achieve an annual aluminum production rate of 300,000 tons. At two-thirds the size of the world's very largest aluminum plant (owned by the Canadian company Alcan), the Alumar complex seemed large by any standard, and large indeed for Maranhão. The operations of the Companhia Vale do Rio Doce, known in Brazil by its initials of CVRD, also sounded substantial, since the terminus of the Carajás railway was there as well as the port. It all struck me as being well worth a new look.

Early on a sunny Sunday morning I was met at the São Luís airport, a rather more contemporary-looking structure than I had remembered, by Tarcísio Araújo Mosci, Alumar's environmental director in Maranhão, and by David Carmichael, an expatriate South African who works for Alumar on personnel and labor-relations matters. "Construction here began in June of 1980, Tarcísio explained as we drove along a smoothly paved highway toward the plant site, which is on the island but eighteen kilometers away from the center of the city. "We started moving earth for the smelter the following year. There are

Alumar's new port at São Luís. This photograph, taken in 1984, shows the first ore carrier to tie up alongside.

ten thousand people working for the various contractors on the job, and 1,200 people working for Alumar directly, as well as several hundred trainees. When we get it finished and running, this place will be a very important factor in the world's aluminum industry. What is happening is that the developed countries are shutting down their aluminum plants. Japan used to have 1.4 million tons a year of domestic capacity. Now they are down to a third of that, and they continue to close down facilities. The same trend is under way in the United States and in Europe. They all face problems of electric power, of which you need an enormous amount to make aluminum. They are all far away from the raw material: bauxite is a tropical mineral that comes out of weathered clay. Their labor costs are rising fast, and they face pollution problems resulting from concentrations of industry. The result of all this is that two countries are emerging as the new great powers in the aluminum world. Australia will serve Japan and the West Coast of the United States. Brazil will serve Europe and the eastern United States. There will be some production in a few other places, like Guyana and Jamaica and Suriname, but we will be the dominant factor in this part of the world."

As Tarcísio finished this sweeping outline, we swung through a gate onto the construction site and along smooth dusty roads of red earth to the port facility. There fast-running water—currents of five to seven knots in the large bay that encircles the island of São Luís—boiled around the great pilings to which ore carriers from Trombetas, as well as other large vessels, have begun to tie up. We followed the large plant through the various stages of smelting and refining, and Tarcísio told me about the various environmental safeguards that the company is applying to the dirty business of making aluminum. To the extent that it is possible, he said, water containing pollutants that emerge during the manufacturing process is kept within a closed system and recycled. All processing areas are diked to avoid runoffs beyond the plant. Excess industrial effluents that cannot be recycled will be piped into a large and elaborate manmade lake whose bottom consists of forty centimeters of nearly impermeable compacted clay. Over this is carefully laid a seamless lining of very tough polyvinyl chloride (PVC). In a further effort to be sure that seepage from the lake is not miraculously occurring, the company has also dug a number of nearby wells and will be continually testing the fresh water in them. The company has sponsored a number of baseline biological inventories and other scientific studies of the region. Although unsophisticated, these have softened some of the opposition. "I've been around aluminum for sixteen years and I've never seen a company that pays so much attention to environmental concerns," said Tarcísio. "This has to come from the top down. Otherwise it simply would not happen."

After a full morning of looking and talking, I was taken to a modern beach-front hotel owned by Editora Abril, a large publishing company based in São Paulo. Smoke was rising from a large barbecue pit beside the kidney-shaped swimming pool, and bikini-clad diners were lining up to receive portions of charred beef and pork and turkey. In this "gold coast" neighborhood were many expensive individual houses and middle-class housing projects. As opposed to my previous trip to São Luís, during which I had seen nothing but slums, I had now been there for fully half a day and had yet to see one. But to remind me of what Maranhão had been, São Luís experienced a power failure that evening, and the hotel kitchen limped along by candlelight. The following morning, when a young Brazilian-American named Paulo Miller showed me the CVRD facilities, I received further confirmation that some of the city's old problems had persisted. The advent of ships and industry, I also learned, had brought some new ones as well.

Since CVRD will do no steel manufacturing at São Luís and will only export iron ore, Miller explained, the company faces no problem of industrial effluents there. Sinterfeed, the kind of iron ore that comes from Carajás, coarse and grainy, will produce little air-polluting dust when the railroad's ore-carrying cars are tipped over and the rock is spilled onto the conveyor belt carrying it to the port and the ships. But Miller worries about the bay. Already, he told me, the large breakwaters that CVRD has built to form its protected port have caused some silting; the long-run consequences remain unknown. And even though few tankers will come to São Luís, oil spillage may become a problem. "Every port is oily," Miller said. "Granted, there is no exact proof that more ships in a port will create more oil. But even a small amount of oil

A traditional fish market in São Luís *(Roger D. Stone)*

Netting shrimp in São Luís. The photograph was taken from a bridge linking the island city with the mainland. *(Roger D. Stone)*

can do a great deal of damage. We have a twenty-one-foot tide and the oil goes down with it and stays on the bottom. Rio de Janeiro's Guanabara Bay is dead, and it died just in the last few years of Rio's revitalization as a port."

Miller's concern for the bay at São Luís is based not on sympathy for the local equivalent of the snail darter, but rather on his appreciation for the fragile *human* ecology in what remains—as it turns out—a highly underprivileged local economy. Despite the new construction jobs, the rush of job-seekers into São Luís has far outpaced the increase in the number of openings. The unemployment rate has remained a staggering fifty percent. Most of those who do have jobs are paid no more than the minimum wage of something like thirty United States dollars per month. Most people in São Luís are highly dependent on what nature can provide, and what nature can most readily provide comes right out of the bay. "The lucky ones," says Miller, "can go out and catch shrimp with a net. It's easy. The current is so fast that all you do is stand there and they swim right in. Those who cannot afford to own a net can sometimes afford to rent one, but if you cannot afford to rent one, what you do is crawl on your belly in the mud to catch crabs." The survival of these precious and free resources is what most concerns Miller about the coming increase in São Luís from a hundred ships a year to about three hundred. In such an ecological confrontation between shrimp and ships, there seems little doubt as to which the winner will be.

Miller worries similarly about several species of fruit that grow in profusion on the lands now occupied by CVRD and by Alumar, that were tended by squatters there, and that constituted an important source of vitamin A for many people with poor diets. "Now," he said, "the fruit comes from farther away and the supply is precarious."

The former squatters themselves were once an issue that polarized and chilled the relations between the town and the companies. In order to proceed with their projects, both were compelled to arrange the eviction from their lands of families of *posseiros* (squatters) who had long been living on them. Elaborate arrangements were made to transfer them to new homesites, but the intended beneficiaries were not impressed. In one instance, the lots offered were smaller than those to be abandoned, and were inadequate for subsistence agriculture or chickens or pigs. Another resettlement plan offered good educational and health-care opportunities but no bus transportation. Despite the care with which the companies tried, at least in some respects, to accomplish the transition, polarization occurred and local politicians were quick to exploit it. Others felt sympathy for the displaced *posseiros*. Warwick Kerr, a former INPA director and expert on bees who now teaches at the federal university in São Luís and works among the people, is among them. "Both companies used the same gangsters to kick out the *posseiros*," he told me. "I go to the same church as these people and I hear the stories every Sunday. The death rate of infants among them has gone way up since they were relocated, and the general state of their health has declined."

How much good, then, will the big new industries do for most of the people in the city of São Luís? Of the 400,000 people who live there, only a few thousand will be directly employed by either of the big companies, although a somewhat wider circle might benefit indirectly from the increase in port activity. The next largest industry is the local brewery, and from there things scale quickly down to the subsistence level. As Miller and Kerr suggest, the cost is considerable as well. For many Maranhenses the net impact is negative. But if there is concern at São Luís about matters of great interest to the populace of the region, the issues remain small-bore in comparison to the Amazonian development project that provokes the greatest anxiety of all: the mammoth dam and hydroelectric scheme at Tucuruí, on the Tocantins River.

This energy engine, ultimately scheduled to produce eight thousand megawatts of electric power, forms the core of the industrial boom that is currently being programmed for eastern Amazonia. Electricity from Tucuruí will run the ore-carrying railway from Carajás to São Luís, and the aluminum refineries at São Luís and at Belém, as well as numerous other mining and mineral ventures that are anticipated. Its cheap hydropower will also replace oil-generated energy for consumer use in Belém and a number of other Amazonian cities at a substantially reduced daily cost. According to one estimate, Tucuruí power will equal what could be generated by burning no less than 400,000 barrels of oil a day. The lake to be created by the Tucuruí dam will eventually flood 2,430 square kilometers of virgin forest, and will at high-water seasons extend almost two hundred kilometers up the Tocantins. Construction on the $5-billion project, which has been under way since 1976, slowed in 1983. The closing of the sluices was pushed back a year. Precisely because of the issues raised by the prospective lake, conservationists breathed temporarily easier.

The problems of Tucuruí are an amalgam of biological risk and bad management; the biological quandary itself is a compound of several serious ecological and health issues. For one thing, Eletronorte—the company that is building and will manage Tucuruí—has made no allowance for the many species of fish that migrate up and down the Tocantins. Though locks will enable relatively large vessels to pass between the lower portions of the river and the lake (not previously possible because of rapids that had existed prior to the construction of the dam), there is no way for the migratory fish to make the passage. Little is known of the habitats or ranges of most of the migratory species in the Tocantins, but many scientists already guess that the overall consequences for aquatic life in the river will be disastrous.

A second problem is the chemistry of the lake. Eletronorte will create it simply by flooding the forest, the vast biomass that is there now. As the trees and plants decompose and release the nutrients stored in them, hydrogen

View from the top of Tucuruí dam before inundation *(Roger D. Stone)*

sulfide bubbling to the surface will create a smell so bad that workers will be forced to wear gas masks. The acidity of the water will increase, perhaps enough to cause corrosion in the turbines or other metal parts of the plant that are exposed to river water. The release of the nutrients will also encourage the growth of aquatic plants, such as the water hyacinth, which proliferate at such a rate that they discourage other forms of life including fish, and whose most effective means of control are defoliants that would themselves poison the water. The creation of the lake will, moreover, bring about favorable breeding conditions for the anopheles mosquito, which carries malaria, as well as for a snail whose larvae transmit schistosomiasis. In the worst case—no one really knows quite what will happen, because so few large hydroelectric projects have ever been undertaken in rain-forest areas—the power station may itself become inoperable because of the chemical conditions that its very construction will have created.

Eletronorte officials tend to wave away these alarming forecasts, mostly on the grounds that the Tocantins flows quite swiftly and that the current will carry away, in manageable increments, all those bad things. Others gravely doubt that it will be so simple. Eneas Salati, a former director of INPA, is one of these. "The decision to do Tucuruí was just as spontaneous as the decision to build the Trans-Amazon Highway," he says. "They never really made an accurate mathematical model, and they have no clear idea of what will happen there." Originally, Eletronorte planned to do no forest clearing prior to the flooding, even though the area contains an estimated 2.8 million valuable hardwood trees. Later, prompted in part by a worrisome environmental assessment statement put together by Robert J. A. Goodland of the World Bank, the company reversed its decision and contracted for some clearing (involving the use of toxic defoliants, among other techniques). CAPEMI, the company to which the contract to extract the timber was issued, had no previous experience at such a task and was riddled with corruption as well. In 1983 it withdrew, having performed at a tortoiselike pace, and Eletronorte itself stepped in to clear some portion of the land before the flood begins. "It's not completely CAPEMI's fault," an Eletronorte engineer named João Basílio told me when I visited Tucuruí early in 1983. "No one had any experience at doing this sort of thing, and the pressure was enormous." The consequences are clear: there will simply not be time for more than a small fraction of the timber to be removed. The best guess that João Basílio could hazard about the ultimate outcome was that although the lake would be lower than the treetops over most of the area, the cutting program had been so organized that the view southward from the top of the dam would be "very clean, beautiful."

João Basílio treated me to an extended tour of the region. We visited the town of Tucuruí, so influenced by the dam that its population has increased tenfold (to about fifty thousand) in just the past few years, and so situated that people who live or work at the bank of the Tocantins during the low-water season get flooded out when the water rises each year and move temporarily elsewhere. We went to a small building in the town that has a simple laboratory for scientists from INPA who from time to time make visits to Tucuruí to study the water and the fishes of the region as well as aquatic vegetation, soils, climate, the degradation of vegetable matter, and other pertinent characteristics of the local ecology. "What we're doing now are baseline studies for the future," João Basílio told me. "We will continue for about five years under the terms of our agreement with INPA, and only then will any results be released." The absence of signs of activity made me wonder how important the findings were likely to be. We went to see the first of the planned twenty-four turbines to be installed at Tucuruí. Fabricated by the French firm of Le Creusot, it had been shipped from Marseilles and had just arrived at the site, where it would be fiberglassed and then installed in its place at the dam. Even without its protective coat, this massive hunk of heavy metal, which weighs 233,000 kilograms, seemed capable of surviving a heavy dose of acid water.

Twenty-six thousand workers had been employed at the height of the frenzied effort to build Tucuruí. The labor force dropped to less than half of that because of the economic crisis, and no more than a couple of thousand people will be needed to run the mighty power plant once it is completed. While I

was there, Eletronorte was beginning to build the permanent town in which
these workers will live, and João Basílio suggested that we go out to have a
look at the "land preparation." We drove along the foot of the dam and it
loomed above us, eighty-six meters in height at its maximum point, and then
plunged into the forest. We proceeded a few kilometers to a place where a
big Caterpillar D-8, its driver caged like a medieval warrior in iron mesh, was
effortlessly brushing aside the tall trees of the forest. Each time a tree fell,
clouds of insects emerged from the rubble, one could only imagine the frantic
flight of the other creatures as they lost their habitat. I photographed the
Caterpillar at work, and wondered at its ability to strip five hectares in a single
day. Then João Basílio, in great excitement, motioned me over to another part
of the widening clearing where a sloth, newly dislodged from a felled tree,
had been leashed to a log by a length of vine attached to one of its front feet.
Five men, two armed with large machetes, surrounded the beast as it struggled
in its efforts to get away. I asked João Basílio what would happen to the sloth.

"*Mata, come,*" he replied—they'll kill it and eat it.

It was not what he said that disturbed me. For many centuries people of
this region have killed and eaten sloths and monkeys. There was no reason to
suppose that the deforestation crew we were watching would behave in any
different way. What impressed me was that even João Basílio, the man in
charge of all forms of environmental protection at Tucuruí, could toss off his
remark with a casual shrug of inevitability. The loss of a sloth seemed a symbol
of all that Tucuruí would cause to perish—the fishes, the forest and the life

Doomed sloth at Tucuruí (*Roger D. Stone*)

Iron mine at Carajás *(Roger D. Stone)*

within it—for the sake of progress. The next morning, flying in an F-27 twin-engined turboprop to Belém over the soggy *várzeas* of the Araguaia-Tocantins valley, I pondered again the question of whose victory would compensate for all these losses.

"What *is* development, anyway?" my wife once asked a wise friend who is an economist.

"An activity," he replied.

If there are distressing aspects both of Tucuruí and of the new installations at São Luís, the Carajás iron-ore mine stands out in refreshing contrast. Even though the task of extracting the iron ore at the remote Serra dos Carajás is relatively clean and the population of the region is low, the government-controlled Companhia Vale do Rio Doce (CVRD), which runs the iron-ore project but has no control over the rest of the sweeping Projeto Grande Carajás, took great pains during the planning stage to build in systems of environmental protection. Before going there, I had heard Maria de Lourdes Davies de Freitas, environmental coordinator at CVRD, deliver a lengthy paper on the subject. She described problems of dust, noise, and other forms of pollution that had plagued the company in its iron-ore export activities in central Brazil. Aware that national sensitivities were rising and that "prevention costs less than cure," CVRD approached the task of Amazonian ore extraction with a built-in bias in favor of environmental protection. Although the sinterfeed to be produced at Carajás tends not to break down into dusty particles while it is being loaded on or off railway cars, there were other issues to reckon with. As it built its mine facilities and its railway and worked toward a production rate of fifteen million tons per year by 1985 (35 million by 1987), the company had to face the consequences of a certain amount of deforestation, the runoff of possibly contaminated water from the mines themselves, and the effect of the Carajás presence and program on a number of Indian groups in the region, of which one had only recently come into contact with the wider world. Within the region to be controlled by the company were an estimated 4,535 Indians in thirty-seven widely scattered villages.

In developing its properties, CVRD's initial reaction was to convene a panel of distinguished scientists to provide advice on environmental matters. (The survival of this advisory group was guaranteed by its inclusion in the provisions of a $300-million loan awarded by the World Bank that forms part of the total $4.5-billion Carajás package.) In 1982 an agreement was signed with the Emílio Goeldi Museum in Belém wherein such scientists as Michael Goulding (on fishes and fisheries), David Oren (on birds), and William Overal (on plants) would go to Carajás to carry out baseline studies. The company also arranged for the government's Indian affairs bureau to assume, with the help of a group of consulting anthropologists, the responsibility of helping the Indians in the region to cope with their new circumstances.

Recently I flew from Rio de Janeiro to Serra Norte, the company town that serves the iron mine, to have a look at the project where construction activities had by now been under way for several years. As my plane came in for a landing, what was most apparent was unbroken, majestic tropical forest stretching to the horizon in all directions. On the ground, my first reaction was surprise at the quality of the air—far cooler and drier than I had usually found in Amazonia. The reason, said Maria de Lourdes's colleague Eduardo Porto, there at the airport to meet and guide me, was simply that Serra Norte was fully six hundred meters above sea level. As for the topography, Eduardo explained, "Where there is iron ore, there is no forest but only scrubby savanna land. To get at the minerals, we do not have to invade the forest but simply pick them up from very close to the surface."

Eduardo and a young English-Brazilian engineer, David Paul Stevens, drove me along a tidy paved road from the airstrip toward a small town. En route, Eduardo pointed out that in order to provide space for electric power lines from Marabá, the closest consequential town, CVRD had been required to cut some strips of forest at the edge of the road. But, he said proudly, the width of these bands had deliberately been left narrower than Eletronorte specifications, and as yet there had been neither problems nor complaints. In town, I saw careful landscaping along the streets. The plants, I learned, came from an experimental garden that Eduardo maintains near the airport. The garden's soil, fairly good to begin with, is enriched with nutrients brought directly from the forest biomass, and only a small proportion of everything planted is not doing well. One side of my guest house, located at the edge of the town, was planted in this manner. On the other side, after crossing a short strip of lawn, I arrived at a small gazebo from which one could look across a valley of unbroken forest. This must, I thought, be the world's most beautiful iron mine.

Later in the day we toured the mine areas, great open pits where the forest suddenly vanishes and is replaced by solid geometric patterns of terraced red earth. Here the ore would be extracted, then placed aboard conveyor belts for sorting and processing en route to the railway depot. About the pits little can be done, Eduardo said; after the ore is removed from them, they will remain forever as scars upon the green landscape. But the water from them will be gathered in reservoirs already built or provided for, and safeguarded there if it is hazardously polluted. As regards the processing stations, however, much of the area will be covered and planted with grasses after construction has been completed. The result will be pleasing aesthetically, and air quality will be maintained because the dust, too, will remain underground. Out of the entire mining concession of 429,000 hectares that CVRD controls, only just

Carajás–São Luís Railway, showing the narrow limits of deforestation to create the right-of-way *(Roger D. Stone)*

a little more than two thousand hectares have had to be cleared for the mines, loading and processing facilities, town, airport, and in fact everything to do with the project except for the railroad right-of-way. It is being cleared to a minimum feasible width of fifty meters to each side of the tracks.

In these and many other ways, Eduardo and his colleagues provided convincing evidence of the environmental care that is being taken at Carajás, a project from which so grand an economic return is also expected. But so that I might glimpse the speed with which the forest can be destroyed when people and activity move in, we also took two trips—one by road, one by helicopter—to lands that lie beyond the company's jurisdiction. Regardless of the new Brazilian policies that control cattle ranching on cleared *hylaea*, the practice continued in the region near Serra Norte that forms part of the zone of influence of the Grande Carajás scheme, whose managers in Brasília are far more influenced by the capital's quick-buck mentality than by the conservationist ethic.

From the air we could see cleared land and ranches in all directions, and the smoke from scores of fires. We flew over Serra Pelada, the famous tiny zone containing a fortune in gold, and saw the busy road commerce between it and a squalid service town with a population of several thousand, which did not exist in 1980. Later I discovered that a government agency called GETAT, under the terms of a contract with Grande Carajás, is in the process of razing some 500,000 hectares for cattle and farming in the region; the idea is to use the land to supply Serra Norte and other mining towns that are expected to be established in the nearby highlands as other projects are launched.

Helicopter and children near Carajás *(Roger D. Stone)*

At one point in our helicopter flight a sudden, violent rain squall forced us to land on the outskirts of a town along the highway from Serra Norte to Marabá. It was not the sort of place where a shiny helicopter sets down every day, and before the rotor stopped turning we could see children running toward us, by the hundreds, from every direction. At the height of the violent rain there must have been five hundred of them in the mud around us, crowding around the aircraft while the pilot frantically sought to prevent them from pulling it apart. They were merely undisciplined and curious, but it was an oppressive, even a harrowing moment. I was relieved when the storm passed and we could lift out of this new, raw place.

At dinner in Carajás, I was joined by a visiting representative of a West German government-controlled development bank. It has relatively little money to lend, the banker explained, and must be highly selective. One of its principal criteria is the degree of environmental quality that any given project displays, and it was largely on these grounds that CVRD's request for a Carajás loan had been favorably received. The banker's remarks confirmed my own positive opinion of the Carajás iron-mining project. Its operations, I had come to feel, would do limited ecological damage relative to the achievement of a major and desperately needed economic return. It was a reasonable tradeoff. Of far greater concern was the apparent lack of environmental control—or even common sense—in regard to the Grande Carajás scheme. The Brazilian economic crisis has slowed it down, and about this one can only be generally pleased. The slower it goes, the more of a chance there is that the "Little Carajás" people can impress the project managers in Brasília with the importance of proper attention to the environment.

Even if the Grande Carajás planners squander forest resources for foolhardy cattle-raising and agricultural ventures, reasons remain to argue that the economic return from the mining activity per se is worth all of the environmental cost involved—including the sheer waste. Heavily dependent on imported oil, Brazil requires further massive amounts of hard currency to service the gigantic foreign debt, which approached $100 billion in 1984. These obligations have compelled Brazil to press hard to achieve rising levels of exports from all possible sources. The record has been impressive: exports of all products rose from only $2.7 billion in 1970 to more than $22.9 billion in 1981—the peak year before collapsing commodity prices caused a temporary drop.

Planners saw the emerging Amazonian mining sector as helping to solve Brazil's balance-of-payments problems in two ways. Imports of basic substances such as aluminum would be replaced by domestic production from the vast Trombetas bauxite reserves. Amazonian minerals and metals would, secondly, make a fast-growing contribution to the nation's total export earnings. With ample supplies of raw materials and an abundance of electricity from Tucuruí, moreover, export-oriented industry would be attracted to the region and also contribute to a favorable balance of payments.

Amazonian mining revenues are enjoying a period of heady growth. In 1977 the principal mining activity in the basin was still Dr. Antunes's manganese venture in Amapá, north of Belém, where the deposits were nearing exhaustion after more than a quarter-century of extraction. Yet that year they represented 55 percent of Amazonia's total mining income of $70 million, and Amazonia that year accounted for no more than 3.21 percent of Brazil's total mineral production. By 1980, thanks largely to the start-up of bauxite shipments from Trombetas, the picture had changed sharply. Amazonian revenues that year reached $450 million, the Amazon's share of national production reached 8.45 percent, and production per capita almost quadrupled. Further projections dwarf even these figures. Even though one result of the national financial crisis of 1982–84 was a slowdown in virtually all Amazonian development activities, it was then being predicted that Amazonian aluminum production would reach the $1-billion level by 1990, when Carajás would produce 50 million tons of ore, generating an additional estimated $870 million. Other Grande Carajás mineral projects—copper, manganese, cassiterite, nickel, and gold—would provide $9.2 billion. Beyond Grande Carajás there was considerable further potential. According to a World Bank estimate, for instance, tin revenues from Rondônia would reach $145 million by 1990. Overall, then, Amazonian mining revenues are expected to pass $10 billion, or more than twenty times the 1980 figure, by the end of the decade.

Relative to other forms of development, mining will not do great ecological harm to the basin. The World Bank ecologist Robert J. A. Goodland went so far as to call it "one of the most appropriate forms of development that are compatible with the environment of Amazonia." Even as harsh a critic of the mining strategy as the University of Illinois sociologist Stephen G. Bunker was able to state, in a recent essay, that "the ecological and demographic disruption caused by mining is small in comparison to that caused by the extension of new roads and by the lumbering and ranching which have followed them. Mining activities are restricted to relatively small areas, and their location depends on geological accident far more than on proximity to roads." Goodland notes the generally high quality of the pollution controls and other measures taken by the Amazonian mining companies generally and M.R.N., the controlling force at Trombetas, in particular.

The principal damage for which the mining industry can be held responsible is a secondhand one: if there were no need for electrical energy to power the big alumina and aluminum refineries, Amazonia would not have to undergo the ecological nightmare of Tucuruí. Yet even taking Tucuruí into account, the overall costs are less ecological than social. For one thing, although construction jobs have brought many itinerant workers into Amazonia, the number of permanent positions will be small, and it is difficult to guess how the labor residue will be absorbed. And while only a relative few are being directly affected by the mining projects, the fact that they are a statistical minority hardly lessens their plight. No matter how hard the shipping companies in the waters around São Luís try to avoid spilling oil, their greatly magnified presence is bound to jeopardize the shrimp fisheries on which the local population so heavily depends. Few of the Indians who have been dislodged because of the construction of the Carajás–São Luís railway will ever get jobs in the mining industry; it will only increase the degree of their dependency on FUNAI, the Indian protection agency. Most broadly, the sociologist Bunker joins more and more intellectuals in Belém and Manaus in arguing, the problem is that Brasília has imposed upon Amazonia a sort of domestic colonialism whose ultimate consequences will be no more favorable for the forgotten *caboclo* than had been the original colonial period or the rubber era. "Development for whom?" many Amazonians are asking about decisions made in Brasília, for there is little or no consultation with institutions or experts within the region. "Minerals projects subvert social and environmental values," says the Amazonian geologist Mário Guerreiro. "The constitution says that these are the people's resources, but look who really benefits." "The Carajás project is a real intervention into our state," said the governor of the state of Pará at a scientific conference in Belém in mid-1983. At the same meeting Lúcio Flávio Pinto, a prolific Belém-born journalist who continues to write for *O Liberal*, the city's leading newspaper, expressed a plea for "a little more sensitivity." "We are getting tired of economic calculations," he said. "Often we Amazonian people feel more like natives in an African colony than like people living in a frontier area that is full of natural resources." Even Clara Pandolfo, the director of the natural resources division of SUDAM, the regional development agency, grumbled to me that the bureaucrats in Brasília "don't understand Amazonia."

The underlying difficulty with an emphasis on mining is the simple fact that mining is extractive; after the extraction is completed, nothing remains. Such are the relations between a peripheral region of the world like Amazonia and the centers of world power and influence, Bunker maintains, that in return for the loss of ecological balance Amazonia has little to look forward to but "progressive underdevelopment." And, he warns, it will happen soon. The Trombetas bauxite holdings are expected to last no longer than sixty-five years; overall, "the recent boom economy may not even last as long as the seventy years which elapsed from the beginnings of the rubber boom in 1840 to its collapse." Bunker's conclusion is stark: "By subordinating the requirements for long-term reproduction of the social and natural environments to immediate political and economic demands for the rapid transformation of natural resources into exportable commodities, government and business threaten an even more profound impoverishment of the Amazon as soon as these resources are exhausted." After the party, in other words, Amazonia may be in for another period of retrenchment and decay as bad as or worse than what followed the rubber boom.

CHAPTER 9

The Balance Sheet

UNTIL THE 1970S, THE MAPPING OF AMAZONIA WAS SKETCHY BY MODERN standards. Then, in 1970, as part of the Program of National Integration, the government launched Projeto Radam, an expensive aerial radar survey conducted principally for the benefit of mining investors and other prospective developers. Radam provided useful information about geology and soils, and data subsequently gathered by means of the LANDSAT remote-sensing program were even more comprehensive and precise. On the basis of information derived from the LANDSAT, Brazil's National Institute for Space Research (INPE) issued in 1980 its first statement about how much of Amazonia had already been deforested by 1978. The magic number, said INPE, was 77,172 square kilometers, or 1.55 percent of the total 4,975,257 square kilometers in the entity called the Legal Amazon. This was obviously a great increase from the 28,595 square kilometers reported as cleared in 1975. But since the percentage figure was still so low, development-minded officials found cause to complain that environmentalists had greatly exaggerated the dangers. Clara Pandolfo, of the Amazon Development Agency (SUDAM), cited and analyzed this figure in a 1982 paper: "It is imperative to put a stop to the sensationalist affirmations by the pseudo-defenders of the Amazon that only seek to confuse public opinion without any technical or scientific background."

The keenest of the "pseudo-defenders" is Phil Fearnside of INPA in Manaus, who for more than a decade has been keeping careful tabs on deforestation in Amazonia. In 1982 he published a detailed reaction to INPE's findings. The limitations of the LANDSAT tended to "underestimate deforestation," he complained, since LANDSAT finds it hard to distinguish between virgin first- and second-growth forest that is more than a few years old. Regions such as the entire Zona Bragantina, whose thirty thousand square kilometers, or more than all of Amazonia that LANDSAT declared as having been deforested in 1975, simply do not get counted. Another scholar, Keith Brown of the University of Campinas in southern Brazil, contested that 8 percent of the basin was in secondary forest before the 1970s surveys ever began. The program has also been criticized for its inability to recognize small areas of deforestation and, as Judith Gunn had told me on the Uaupés, is not able to penetrate through cloud cover. These and other considerations have persuaded many serious scientists that the official figures are grossly underestimated and that 10 percent or more of the original forest has probably already disappeared; the most radical estimate is 25 percent. Even the official figure, based on a combination of the 1978 LANDSAT data and more recent surveys, has risen to 2.4 percent.

More worrisome than the amount of Amazonia that has been felled is the rapid acceleration in the rate of deforestation. In a recent paper, Fearnside compared INPE's figures for 1975 with its figures for 1978. Using a carefully designed formula, he suggested an "exponential" increase in the rate averaging 33 percent a year and peaking at 41 percent in Rondônia. If his calculations were correct, the forest in Rondônia will have been fully cleared by 1988; all but small fragments of the Amazonia forest will have vanished by the end of the century. Other scientists support Fearnside's hypothesis. "The overall rate varies," said INPA's Herbert Schubart, "but there is no doubt that in some places it is exponential and in these places we can really predict disaster soon." Not even the economic downturn has had much of an effect, adds Eneas Salati: "Even though officials deny it, everybody knows that the deforestation rate is increasing. The economic crisis has only decreased the rate of increase." Ultimately, says Fearnside, "It doesn't really matter how long it takes. The important question is simply that of whether or not you deforest. If you want to stop, you have to make a conscious decision to do so. Otherwise the process is inexorable."

What does this really mean? To appreciate the answers, one must first place Amazonia's importance in the hemispheric and then in the global context. The Brazilian forest represents some eighty percent of the whole of the Amazonian *hylaea*, which in turn represents close to half of the world's entire remaining

Deforestation in Amazonia. A large bulldozer can fell four to
five hectares a day. *(Roger D. Stone)*

ten million square kilometers of moist tropical forest. Pressures on the African
and Asian forests are far more severe than on Amazonia, because of greater
population densities and conditions more favorable than Amazonia's for log-
ging and other extractive activities; far higher percentages of them have already
been lost than even the most extravagant projections would show for Amazonia. In short, it can safely be assumed that if the Amazonian forest disappears,
virtually all the rest of the world's supply of this sort of forest will already
have vanished. It can happen with lightning speed. After only thirty years of
intensive cutting for mining and farming and towns between 1950 and 1980,
during which far and away a greater part of the damage was done than during
the colonial period and the early decades of the twentieth century, Brazil's
Mata Atlântica (coastal forest) was reduced to no more than two percent of
its original size. If Fearnside's calculations prove correct, Rondônia will be
stripped in but half that time. Overall, it will have taken human locusts only
half a century to destroy what in 1952, when P. W. Richards published his
classic study of the tropical forest, constituted half of all the world's woodlands.

Such an occurrence would be a profound tragedy for mankind and the
planet—one that, because of its irreversibility in less than millions of years,
the Harvard sociobiologist E. O. Wilson has said would be a greater disaster
than "energy depletion, economic collapse, limited nuclear war, or conquest
by a totalitarian government." He and many other natural scientists have come

to feel that tropical forests are all but sacred places.

So much has been said and written about the reasons for their general importance to the stability and well-being of the planet that I will here attempt no more than a brief review. One principal set of hypotheses has to do with the forest's effect on the mixture of gases in the atmosphere. At one time it was widely believed that through photosynthesis the tropical forest was a major contributor of oxygen. This, however, turns out to be a canard, because the forest consumes, through the oxidation of its own dead matter, as much as it produces. Says the ecologist Herbert Schubart: "We'll die of hunger before we'll be asphyxiated." A more serious question involves carbon dioxide, whose atmospheric concentration has been steadily rising for the past quarter-century, thanks largely to motor vehicles and industry. When tropical forest is felled and burned, the vast amount of carbon stored in its biomass is also released into the atmosphere. Deforestation has thus become a fast-growing contributor to the increase in the atmospheric "carbon budget." In turn, according to a well-publicized warning issued by the U.S. Environmental Protection Agency in 1983, the resulting carbon buildup is likely to produce a "greenhouse effect" that could result in significantly warmer temperatures on earth before the end of the century. Polar ice would melt, water levels would rise sharply, and many of the earth's most productive lands would be inundated. Another atmospheric condition, still poorly understood, has to do with nitrous oxide, which is an important factor in regulating the earth's radiation, heat balance, and ozone layer. Tropical agricultural practices, including deforestation, may contribute to an increase in atmospheric nitrous oxide, whose consequences for the planet could include changes in the ozone layer and in ultraviolet light radiation.

While some scientists believe in the correlation between deforestation in the tropics and changes in the very atmosphere that governs life on earth, others suggest that too little is yet known for any consequential conclusions to be reached. Some even suggest that a warmer earth would benefit agriculture by enabling plants to grow faster. But if there are uncertainties about the function of carbon and nitrogen in setting global climatic conditions — and about what the tropical forest does to establish the growing levels of both substances — the relationship between rain and the tropical forest is more clearly understood. Fully half of Amazonia's rainfall, as we have already learned, consists of moisture released into the atmosphere by evapo-transpiration from the trees themselves. Each clearing made in the forest, then, results in an incremental loss of moisture. For this reason, said the scientists Lovejoy and Salati in a 1982 paper, no more dramatic a change in Amazonia than a series of small clearings "can in the aggregate be a matter of real concern." The clearing of larger areas is already known to affect the amount of local rainfall; the growth of Manaus, for instance, has doubtless made the city warmer and drier. In 1979, the limnologist Harald Sioli reported that for the first time in recorded weather history it simply did not rain there for six solid weeks. "That was just incredible," says Judy Rankin. "We have a pronounced dry season anyway. Prolonging it by a month and a half almost takes us out of the evergreen rain forest class. That would be a very serious change for us. Where I live there is a lot of forest still, and we have a couple of hundred hectares of lightly logged forest between us and the city. At our house there is mist in the morning, and I can tell you how far into Manaus I can drive before I run out of the mist. It's tree cover, that's all." The rate of change varies in close proportion to the amount of deforestation. "The possibility of a drying trend in Amazonian climate," Lovejoy and Salati argue, "is a threat to any biologically based undertaking in the basin."

Speculation is also mounting that flooding, a known consequence of deforestation on other continents, is also beginning to affect Amazonia. Along the waterfront of Manaus there is a register showing the height of high water during each flood season since the 1920s, and the range—perhaps ten meters—is impressive. Even though variations were wide before serious deforestation began in the region, some scientists, including particularly Alwyn Gentry of the Missouri Botanical Garden, suspect that it has been a principal cause of unusually high flood levels in recent years. "I've been saying for a long time that the clearing for the Trans-Amazon and the other highways would potentially cause more runoff and flooding on the Amazon, and perhaps leave the *várzea* permanently underwater or destroy it," says the anthropologist Betty Meggers. "When we last went up the river, in September 1982, they had one of the highest water levels in history during the most recent rainy season. It had ended, but the current was still very strong and the water higher than usual. Whether this was a natural phenomenon, say a fifty-year occurrence, or whether it was provoked by all this cutting, is something we will only know over the next several years. If the trend continues, we'll soon begin to see the sort of impact I've been thinking about."

Another familiar argument in favor of preserving the tropical forest suggests the madness of destroying species before they have even been discovered, let alone examined for their possible contributions to human wealth or well-being. We have already reviewed the ways in which wild plants contribute to human health. Their germ plasm has helped to protect many common species of food plant from disease or virus. The perfume and fragrance industries are highly dependent on products to be found only in the tropical forest. Margery L. Oldfield, a biologist at the University of Texas, reminds us that until 150 years ago, rubber was regarded as a curiosity without economic importance. Had Amazonia then been clear-cut, as were the eastern woodlands of the United States at the time, *Hevea brasiliensis* might easily have succumbed to extinction before its immense value had become known. The same is in all probability true of countless other still-undiscovered species in what Oldfield called the vast "genetic reservoir" of the tropical rain forest.

To be important to the well-being of the ecosystem, a species does not necessarily have to be a star in its own right; there are many bit players whose roles are essential to other more impressive actors. Robert Goodland and his co-author, Howard Irwin, put it this way in their slim but influential 1975 volume, *Amazon Jungle: Green Hell to Red Desert?*:

> The importance for preserving undiscovered species from extinction lies in their role in the ecosystem: different plants in the forest depend on each other and are functionally linked with insects and animals. A certain species of plant may not in itself be of recognized economic importance to man, but it may provide the food for an insect species which at another time of year pollinates the flowers of a tree of importance. There are many other obligate interactions within the forest between the plants and insects, birds, bats and rodents.... Until more is known...about the balance of nature within the forest, it is courting disaster to cut over large areas.

"There are a million species out here," says as scientist working in one corner of Amazonia, "and only five of us." In Belém, David Oren has been studying a number of common species of Amazonian parrot, whose large populations and bright colors make them among the most obvious residents of the forest. Yet Oren has discovered fundamental errors in the literature about the basic biology of these birds—their range, feeding and breeding habits. "In ornithology here, even at its best, we're about where U.S. ornithology was in the 1930s," he says. "Overall, we're still back in the nineteenth century." If interest in the natural science of the tropics has been growing of late, the gaps are still enormous. Academia still emphasizes the temperate regions of the planet. Even among the relatively few scientists trained to do fieldwork in the tropics, many would prefer other sorts of work. There is disease and discomfort in the field, and the financial and professional rewards are greater for many who stay closer to the power centers. Progress toward new scientific knowledge is often frustratingly slow, therefore, and scientists the world over plead for time.

"Biology...has come a long way since pre-Darwinian times," wrote Meggers in a recent paper, "but we are only beginning to appreciate the marvelous intricacy of the genetic code, the astounding diversity of living things, and the amazing complexity of ecosystems. Ecologists, agronomists, climatologists, and others who attempt to synthesize knowledge about climates, soils, crops, and fuels, and to predict the impact of technological manipulations and inputs can only issue warnings because, although all organisms affect their surroundings, none before us appears to have altered conditions irreversibly on a planetary scale at so rapid a rate." Other voices call for time not only for the sake of discovery or of pure science, and not only on the grounds that what they discover may directly contribute to human well-being, but on a loftier plane as well. In moral or ethical terms, they ask, and I join them: How can man justify the willful and near-instant destruction of our greatest cathedral, a monumental work whose construction, by millions of different forms of life, required millions of painstaking years?

In response to these and other powerful arguments in favor of tropical forest preservation and of greater attention paid generally to environmental matters, Brazilian attitudes have changed sharply. At the 1972 Stockholm Conference on the Human Environment, the Brazilian delegation was the world's least conservation-minded. Those who represented the Brazilian Miracle, then in full swing, carried with them a simple message: "Send us your pollution. We need the jobs." It was not long before enthusiastic responses to this request had caused air pollution to rise to disagreeable levels in industrial São Paulo; a toxic-waste scandal, clearly attributable to carelessness as well as to a dangerous overconcentration of chemical plants, erupted in the smaller city of Cubatão. Deforestation was increasing dramatically within Amazonia and beyond. Oil began to wash up on the beaches.

Public complaints mounted steadily through the 1970s. The press, increasingly free as Brazilian governance gradually shifted from the hard-line dictatorship of President Emílio Garrastazu Médici (1969–77) to a more open system, saw environmental issues as a convenient way to express opposition to the regime. The public—like the public elsewhere, as with the Green political movement in West Germany—followed suit. Newly unmuzzled opposition politicians gleefully seized upon the government's deal with D. K. Ludwig as a flagrant symbol of a flawed policy, and it became a hotly debated *cause célèbre*. In southern Brazil, a network of somewhat left-wing "Committees for the Defense of Amazonia" was formed to oppose the government's Amazonian policies, which they viewed as designed only to benefit powerful entrepreneurs from southern Brazil and multinational corporations. Exploitation and mistreatment of the dwindling Indian population became a national issue of scandal proportions, culminating in the election to the national congress in 1982 of Mário Juruna, a full-blooded Indian chief, whose accusations and denunciations received broad international and intense local coverage.

In Brasília, though overall policies were slow to reflect the changing public mood about environmental questions, there eventually came some indications of official rethinking. In 1974 a mild-mannered aristocrat, Paulo Nogueira Neto, quietly took office as the Special Secretary for the Environment, a newly created cabinet-level position that Brazil never thought it would need; in 1980 he was appointed to a second six-year term. With calm effectiveness Nogueira and his small staff have since been working to introduce environmental considerations into development planning, and to protect biologically important regions from ill-considered incursions. Another public agency that also came alive during the 1970s was the Brazilian Institute for Forest Development, whose parks division was led until late 1982 by the fiery and effective Maria Teresa Jorge Pádua, whose efforts to protect Amazonia provided an immediate reason for Lovejoy's research. Cajoling and badgering and wheedling, Maria Teresa (as she is universally known) fought long odds to bring about a major expansion in the dimensions of the existing system of national parks and forest reserves. During her term in office, she pulled some seven million hectares into the Amazonian parks network. Even though management of these reserves was skimpy for budgetary reasons, their mere delineation was an important milestone—particularly in view of the close correlation between park sites and the biologically diverse "refuges" where species congregated during the Pleistocene ice ages.

At the same time that public and official interest were growing, scientific knowledge of the realities and the sharp limitations of Amazonia rapidly increased. Scientists are quick to point out that only a tiny fraction of what there is to be learned about the forest is now known, and they plead for time. But the growth in knowledge, particularly of the forest's vulnerability, has been striking. "Ten years ago," says Judith Gunn, "there were mostly suspicions. Now it's mostly documented." The lengthening list of project failures—from the end of the natural-rubber era to the demise of the Henry Ford rubber operations, from the mid-1970s collapse of the cattle industry at Paragominas to Ludwig's *gmelina* difficulties—cause doubts about the economic viability of unsubsidized Amazonian investments.

Investors have balked not only because of previous failures, but also because of the sheer cost of getting things done in Amazonia. Transportation requires fossil fuel, and much of what is commonly used in Amazonia, including many basic foodstuffs and other everyday commodities, is shipped in from far away; so much for living off the bountiful land, as the Omáguas did. High costs, which slowed the big Amazonian development projects when the Brazilian economy ran into heavy weather in the 1980s, may inhibit Amazonian "progress" over the longer term as well. "When you consider the economic costs and not just the financial costs," says Robert Skillings of the World Bank, "most of these big Amazonian operations are probably losing money in real terms. The real constraint is that the costs here are at least forty percent higher than the national average. So investments are only viable if the government provides subsidies, and these are becoming scarcer as the economic crisis deepens. I see these natural forces as pointing to rather slow growth for Amazonia."

A certain skepticism among public and private international investors about Amazonia's development potential began in the mid-1970s when Goodland, formerly a professor of environmental science at McGill University and an ecologist at the New York Botanical Garden, published his shrill book and, soon after, became the World Bank's environmental specialist. Though still accused of insensitivity by many conservationists, the World Bank has been affected at least somewhat by Goodland's warnings. Its loans to Amazonian projects now routinely include provisions for environmental research, Indian protection, or both. The shift in the Bank's policy has had a "ripple effect" among industrial investors, Alcoa for one, although commercial banks still tend to view the borrower's credit-worthiness as the sole criterion for loans even to such risky Amazonian ventures as cattle ranching or plantation agriculture.

Overall, the changing public mood and economic conditions have created an improving climate for a more balanced Amazonian development policy. A decade ago, apart from Indian protection measures that had ecologically favorable components, there was little to protect Amazonia from human predation other than Maria Teresa's parks-expansion program and the widely abused and defective rule saying that an Amazonian landowner could clear no more than half of his property. Later, however, came official recognition that Amazonian cattle projects were not sufficiently successful to justify the lavish fiscal incentives that had been set up to encourage their creation. New guidelines published by SUDAM, the regional development agency, stress the better conditions to be found on the vast (more than a million square kilometers) and underpopulated *cerrado* or savanna lands on the central plateau south of Amazonia. Lessons learned by the failures of the small-farmer colonization efforts of the early 1970s led to a wiser new effort called POLAMAZONIA that would emphasize development in certain parts of the basin and environmental protection elsewhere. In 1979 President Ernesto Geisel announced yet another new Amazon policy that would be based upon the twin pillars of economics and ecology in full recognition of the region's vastness and diversity; various ministries and government agencies were told to submit proposals suggesting policy details, and some—notably INPA and SUDAM—did so. On the basis of these the government prepared a draft law with important environmental-protection provisions, and submitted it to a congressional commission for review. The bill remains tabled there—a victim of bureaucratic inertia and of the shift from the Brazilian Miracle to an economic crisis. Sadly, many Brazilians are again thinking less about sustainable resource use than about quick returns.

Yet the government rhetoric, meanwhile, remains strong in its commitment to conservation as well as to surmounting debt, inflation, and unemployment. In 1982, at a ceremony in Brasília to present an international conservation award to Paulo Nogueira Neto and Maria Teresa Jorge Pádua, President Figueiredo went out of his way to denounce those who would exploit the Amazon basin's resources in a "predatory" way. The ecologist Herbert Schubart was relieved. "The tractor was an economic concept completely misadapted to ecological conditions in Amazonia," he says. "Fortunately, it looks as though our tractor era is ending."

The time has arrived, in short, when an observer of the unfolding drama might dare to dream that rational and balanced policies could channel Amazonian development in the future. At the very least, science and experience and political reality all point to ready conclusions about what an acceptable and ecologically sound program would be. No strategy that does not emphasize the mining sector, whatever its long-term shortcomings, would currently pass muster in Brasília. Timber, rubber, and Brazil nuts are other Amazonian products whose controlled harvest from the wild would provide a living for future generations of *caboclos*. The anthropologist Charles Wagley, a doyen of research in Amazonia, supports the model. "For good or bad," he argues, "you're not going to keep development out. I'm against the extreme environmentalists who just want to close the whole place up. That's just not realistic. But I do wonder whether the small farmer can make it in Amazonia beyond the subsistence level. During the next century, I hope, we'll see more agricultural research and some science that will tell us how to make agroforestry and silviculture work. Meantime, the region will have to get along, somehow, on the basis of minerals and hydroelectric power."

Harvesting rice on deforested land *(Roger D. Stone)*

Against the extractive impulse, then, can be set an agricultural policy stressing agroforestry, silviculture, and other sustainable plantation schemes—only where favorable conditions exist. Here Amazonians could replicate the Yurimaguas model for commercially scaled farming activities. On *várzea* lands, rice and seasonal vegetable production would be stressed. Means could be found to end the plundering of the fisheries, and to install aquaculture activities where possible. As for most conventional forms of agriculture, João Murça Pires's strategy of nondevelopment is probably the correct government policy. Road-building would have to be curtailed, and under all but very unusual circumstances prospective colonists would be encouraged to settle not within the Amazonian heartland, but on the usually less populated and more productive *cerrados*. (Disincentives for population growth in Amazonia, except in designated areas such as Rondônia where it is inevitable, would be worked out.) Consideration might even be given to the fulfillment of Betty Meggers's old dream of piping Amazonian water into Brazil's parched northeast, whose soils are relatively good, rather than trying to tear the Nordestinos away from their land and relocate them in barren Amazonia. Properly managed parks and protected areas, and the sustainable use of all resources, should be highlighted.

Realistically, though, policies of this sort are hardly likely. For one thing, though this may be the least important consideration for the longer term, money for conservation is in far shorter supply than money for development. For example, plans for the Tapajós National Park, near Itaituba, provided for a staff of 250 people and a handsome new headquarters complex atop a rise with a commanding view of the forest and the river. When I went there recently, I was greeted by a total staff of six spirited but overwhelmed workers; the rangers were unable to carry out their basic border patrol program. Poaching was on the rise and squatters were pushing in. All that existed of the proposed headquarters was a flattened bare area on the hilltop. The departing construction crew had abandoned a water-tank car, and weeds and vines were symbolically growing over it. "Someday they will build the headquarters," said one of the rangers. "The question is—which century?"

If money were more plentiful for conservation, it would also be more plentiful for development. Yet the lack of it is probably less of a hindrance to the organization of a sound program for Amazonia than are human factors such as administrative disarray and the sheer difficulty of getting things done in a vast and primitive place. Little technical assistance is available to Amazonian farmers, for instance, simply because of bureaucratic shortcomings. "The government does some fairly good research," says João Murça Pires. "But the results never get out to the people. They only go to Brasília and get filed there." Communications remain primitive outside Amazonia's largest towns. Boundaries, registers, and maps are in short supply, cases of fraud are commonplace, and there are endless disputes about titles and ownership; the widespread confusion about land tenure hinders the evolution of rational policies, and encourages unproductive deforestation. (Most harmful is the time-honored Amazonian practice of considering land as being "improved" or "in use" after deforestation, and thus the rightful property of the occupant rather than of the government, which theoretically owns all unused property in the region. Naturally, this doctrine provides subsistence-level squatters and big entrepreneurs alike with a strong incentive to clear as much land as possible.) "The problem of land titles," says Wagley, "probably causes as much human misery as anything in Amazonia."

An equally powerful constraint is that people in Amazonia, perhaps like people everywhere, tend to resist change stubbornly, even if new opportunities or technologies become available. Many of the colonists entering Rondônia, where technical assistance is becoming readily available thanks to the Polonoroeste program, have nonetheless practiced traditional and wasteful methods of agriculture and cattle-raising. The more people pour into Amazonia and attempt conventional slash-and-burn agriculture, the less success they will have. In the old days, Indian farmers shifted their *roças* (farm sites) as they exhausted the nutrients, and every eight or ten years moved their entire villages and began to work virgin lands. Already, in some parts of Amazonia, farmers are returning to the same *roças* after leaving them fallow for only three years; at the "Amazon Town" that Wagley has studied since the 1940s, the only crop that survives under these conditions is manioc. As the yields decline, Amazonians will be forced to push even farther into the forest in search of new lands, and the "opening up" process will continue inexorably. Even as things are, *caboclos* have already grabbed up most of the good land; the colonists entering from the south or northeast have to do with what's left.

Given a choice between one meal and no meals at all, most people will understandably opt for the meal. Even if it is the very last to be had, an alligator skin or a jaguar pelt will provide that meal. A hungry poacher is not likely to worry much about whether his prey's species is endangered or not. If a tree or a plant in the forest has economic value, Amazonians are likely to exploit it until it disappears. And this is true at the policymaker's level as well. Such are the pressures in Brazil to create jobs and revenues and export earnings that the principles of sustainability are often deliberately defied in order to achieve the one-time-only benefit. "Conservation education" efforts to persuade citizens that the resources around them have more value preserved than squandered have worked in other countries. But there is no such thing in Amazonia, and little likelihood that one, if mounted, would have prompt or significant results.

Not even today, moreover, is there agreement among the leadership about what constitutes wise policy. Late in 1982, Maria Teresa Jorge Pádua went to Bali to attend an important international parks conference. In her absence, the minister to whom she was reporting ruled in favor of building a road that neatly bisects one of her Amazonian parks, reportedly at the suggestion of "powerful timber interests." When she returned to Brasília, Maria Teresa submitted her resignation in protest, reckoning that such a dramatic gesture would compel the minister to rescind his order. Instead, he let it stand. "He would have been crazy to do otherwise," a São Paulo businessman with Amazonian investments told me. "Going through the park shortens the trip by four hundred kilometers." The road is under construction. Maria Teresa has a less powerful new job in São Paulo. The fortunes of IBDF, never politically strong, have declined as economic pressures have grown. If their original positions in favor of all-out development have softened, such agencies as SUDAM and EMBRAPA have hardly become fully converted to a conservationist strategy.

If the Amazonian forest disappears, it is likely that all the other tropical forests of the planet will have preceded it over the horizon. If any tropical forest in the world is redeemable, on the other hand, it is the Amazonian forest—the world's largest and least ravaged and biologically most important. At the very least, it might be possible to avoid the ultimate irony, as Lovejoy and Schubart stated in a recent article, of the basin's becoming "one enormous enterprise in hydroponics." But sharp and unlikely changes in Brazilian attitudes and performance will be required. And non-Brazilians will have to realize that whatever they do will have little influence. Does this mean that all "we" can do is watch while the game is played out? Quite to the contrary. There are many ways in which the United States and other nations can develop and promulgate attitudes, policies, and programs that would make it more likely that Brazil will conserve Amazonia instead of squandering it.

For one thing, it will be useful to continue to provide educational opportunities—everything from full-fledged graduate programs to shorter seminars in wildlife or parks management—for Brazilian scientists, and to find ways to support the few Brazilian institutions (e.g., the Museu Emílio Goeldi and INPA) that specialize in tropical science. Since there will be a continuing need for collaborative research efforts such as Lovejoy's project, educational institutions in the industrial world must place a greater emphasis on the tropics—and on the sharp differences between tropical ecosystems and those of the temperate zones. In the United States, we need entire institutions devoted to the subject, not just a few dedicated individuals.

The structure of U.S. economic policies will also have great importance for Amazonia. The harder or more protectionist the U.S. policy line with regard to trade arrangements and debt service, the more Brazilians will feel obliged to plunder the Amazon for nonrecurring profit. Although the United States conducts no AID program in Brazil (Brazil is considered too "developed" to require such assistance), the agency is already providing indirect assistance through support of several tropical-science research activities, and should do more of this. AID has also begun to think more about the environmental consequences of all its programs; its new concern could influence other U.S. government and private institutions that work in Brazil. How private foreign investors behave in Amazonia matters—although it is preferable that the issue remain one of corporate conscience rather than of legislative fiat.

In several respects, it will be important for the United States to maintain and even strengthen various laws that affect Amazonia. The Endangered Species Act, which has often come under heavy pressure since it was enacted in

Survivor *(Roger D. Stone)*

1973, is a leading example. The list of endangered species, maintained under the terms of that law, serves as the principal working document for the global Convention on International Trade in Endangered Species (CITES), which offers protection to many Amazonian species, from orchids to spotted cats, that are in heavy international demand. The rigor of other U.S. laws, including those regulating beef imports and controlling exports of hazardous products such as chemical defoliants, directly affects the Amazonian condition.

Internationally, we must hope, the World Bank will encourage fainter-hearted agencies such as the Inter-American Development Bank, UNCTAD, and the United Nations Development Program to take stronger positions on tropical-forest issues. At the Bank, even the vigilant Goodland is only one of many voices, and he hardly wins all arguments. Despite the research pointing to the importance of developing the bordering *cerrados* rather than the heartland of Amazonia, it was disheartening to learn that the Bank was only "just beginning to think" about the question in 1984. In all likelihood, the urgent need to find employment for the world's poor will long overshadow in the Bank's mind the threat that development poses to the planet's ecology. Yet Goodland's mere presence on the scene, and the small victories he has won in getting environmental provisions into the Polonoroeste loan package and elsewhere, represent an important if fragile beginning.

At bottom, though, the chances of an ultimate victory seem remote. The villain of the piece is not voracious capitalism among multinational corporations, or heartless São Paulo entrepreneurs, or runaway technocracy in Brazil's military and civilian planning and development agencies. It is, rather, human nature itself. The notion of Amazonian development continues to be as fundamental to Brazilian thinking as was that of westward expansion in the United States of a century ago—"our moon shot," one Brazilian said. That Amazonian development schemes have so often failed only adds spice to the challenge in a land where *machismo* still reigns and where issues are still decided more often at the point of a gun than in a courtroom. The continuance of explosive population growth in the basin seems as inevitable as it is undesirable, and the people who come there in search of new El Dorados will have to discover different means of survival after the treasure is exhausted. Brazil, a land of great intelligence and humor and style, seems to lack the overall will to rise to the challenge of putting Amazonian occupation on a rational and sustainable basis. The disappearance of Amazonia's forests will be gradual but inexorable, and there is precious little that anyone beyond Brazil can do about it.

PRONUNCIATION GUIDE

PORTUGUESE, IT IS SAID, IS AS CLOSE AS ANY MODERN LANGUAGE TO THE colloquial Latin of Roman soldiers. The Brazilian version has been enriched by the incorporation of many Indian words (e.g., the beverage called *xibé*) and slang expressions.

Although Portuguese speakers have little difficulty understanding Spanish, the reverse is not usually the case, and one of the reasons is the considerable complexity of Portuguese pronunciation. In this regard, the Brazilian styles (of which there are many, and all very different from how the language sounds in Portugal) are particularly hard to decipher. The acute accent mark (′) serves as a guide as to where to stress accented words. The name *Emílio*, for example, is pronounced EmEE-lio.

What follows is a short list of how to pronounce a few of the tricky words most often used in this volume. Plesae note that Spanish pronunciations (e.g., *Acuña* is Ah-COON-ya) are omitted, and everything below is Portuguese.

Aldeia: Al-DAYA
Belém: Bay-LAIN

Cachaça: Ca-SHASSA

Cuiabá: Coo-ya-BAH

João: The *j* is a soft *zh* sound, as in the French word *jeudi*, and the *oão* rhymes with *wow*. Note that the soft *j* applies to all words beginning with that letter: *Juscelino*, *Juruá*, etc.

Manaus: Man-AUS. The last three letters rhyme with *house*.

Maranhão: Maran-YOW.

Negro: The *eg* is pronounced like *egg*.

Noronha: No-RON-ya.

Santarém: Santa-RAIN.

São: Gringos usually try to pronounce this "say oh," but that's not right. The precise inflection is not easy to put into phonetics, but it more or less rhymes with *wow*, as in the *João* example above.

Solimões: Soli-MOYS.

Tapajós: Once again, note the soft *j*, and it's a long *o*, as in the word *those*. Tapa-ZHOS.

Uaupés: Wow-PAYS.

Várzea: VAR-zia.

Velho. Once again, the gringo version is VEL-hoe. The right form, however (see *Noronha*), is VEL-yow.

Xingu. The *x* is almost like the *j*, a soft *zh* sound.

A final word about people's names. These are quite fanciful in Brazil, and they come from all over. There are many Brazilians with first names from Greco-Roman or American history (Euclides, Hermongenes, many Roosevelts and Wilsons) and some, as in the former federal deputy named Dix-huit Rosado, from sheer caprice and the good or bad fortune to have been someone's eighteenth child. In conversation, many Brazilians refer to one another by their first names. "Bon dia, Senhor Roger," a Brazilian would probably say to me— not "Bon dia, Senhor Stone." I have tended to use last names in my text, with one important exception: where the final word in the name is *neto*, as in Antonio Delfim Neto. *Neto* means "grandson," and to refer to Mr. Delfim as "Mr. Neto" would be like calling Sammy Davis, Jr., "Mr. Junior." The same is true of the Portuguese word *filho*, meaning "son," which is often part of a man's name. *Filho* is pronounced FIL-yow.

NOTES

CHAPTER 1

Though personal experience provided almost all of the material for this chapter, it also contains references to the journals of four earlier voyagers who ventured near or into the Uaupés: Baron Alexander von Humboldt, Richard Spruce, Henry Walter Bates, and Alfred Russel Wallace. With regard to the thoughts and observations of Judith Gunn, the graduate student who is frequently mentioned in the narrative, it should be recorded that her doctoral thesis supervisor at the University of Wisconsin is William Denevan, the author of a paper listed in the bibliography and the scholar who suggested that Amazonia during the pre-Hispanic period may have supported a far larger human population than has commonly been estimated until recent years.

CHAPTER 2

An interview with Norman Newell, the distinguished paleontologist at the American Museum of Natural History, provided the latest scientific comment on the material about Amazonia's geological history that opens this chapter. Information was also culled from the *Hammond World Atlas* and from the

International Geographic Encyclopedia and Atlas, as well as from early sections of the anthropologist and archaeologist Betty J. Meggers's pioneering book, *Amazonia: Man and Culture in a Counterfeit Paradise*. Caryl P. Haskins's thorough history, published in 1943 and called *The Amazon: A Life History of a Mighty River*, contains a useful description of the formation of the basin. So does an article by James J. Hester about the late Pleistocene period.

As suggested in the text, no contemporary book dwelling on the European discovery and exploration of the region is more enlightening or entertaining than *The Southern Voyages*, the second of the two-volume series by the late Samuel Eliot Morison of Harvard. Another seminal work consulted with regard to this period is Edward J. Goodman's *The Explorers of South America*, which covers them all from Columbus to Colonel Fawcett, the British adventurer who disappeared in the interior of Mato Grosso early in the twentieth century. No less important a reference is the widely cited *Red Gold: The Conquest of the Brazilian Indians 1500–1760* by John Hemming of the Royal Geographical Society in London. Friar Carvajal's account of Orellana's descent of the Amazon is indispensable; an anthology entitled *South from the Spanish Main*, edited by Earl Parker Hanson and published in 1967, provides snippets from other early chronicles.

CHAPTER 3

Research for this chapter, as well, was divided between narratives of journeys and the more analytical work of latter-day historians. Humboldt's extensive writings were consulted, as were the words and remarkable illustrations that emerged from Alexandre Rodrigues Ferreira's *Viagem Filosófica* and Father Acuña's sprightly prose. David Graham Sweet's doctoral dissertation about seventeenth-century Amazonia contains vivid and extensive documentation of how grim things were during the early colonial period, and of the heroic efforts that individuals such as Father Fritz along the upper Solimões and Father Vieira in Pará made to improve relations with the Indian populations. *Four Centuries of Portuguese Expansion*, by the influential British historian C. R. Boxer, illuminates the relationship between the court in Lisbon and the colonies in Brazil. The Haskins, Hemming, Hanson, and Goodman volumes all enriched this portion of the story; the article by the Reverend George Edmundson illuminates the role of Pedro de Teixeira in the Portuguese occupation of Amazonia and subsequent expansion into the basin.

CHAPTER 4

When I first began to do systematic research toward the preparation of this book, an early and important call was at the office of Ghillean T. Prance, Senior

Vice-President for Science at the New York Botanical Garden and a veteran student of the flora of Amazonia. When I asked Prance what I should read, he unhesitatingly replied, "Bates, Spruce, Wallace." "What else?" I recall asking. "Spruce, Wallace, Bates," Prance said. "Do that and then we can talk some more." So it was that I was wisely led to the material forming the heart of this chapter, and of thinking about Amazonia on the part of almost all scientists and naturalists from then until very recent times. Other journals cited are those of the Bavarian scientists von Spix and von Martius and of Professor and Mrs. Agassiz.

The anthropologist Charles Wagley, for many years affiliated with Columbia University and now at the University of Florida (Gainesville) contributed much information for this chapter. *Amazon Town*, his classic study of the village of Gurupá on the lower Amazon which was first published in 1953, contains moving paragraphs about how the passing of the rubber era affected life in this isolated community. The various chapters of a sweeping anthology called *Man in the Amazon*, edited by Wagley in the early 1970s, were a rich lode for many parts of my story but particularly for its coverage of developments in the basin late in the nineteenth century through to the 1960s. Many books, articles, and journals (as well as some accounts that are more fanciful than credible) contributed to my understanding of the stress and splendor of the rubber era.

CHAPTER 5

The Nevins and Hill biography of Henry Ford, published in 1957, yielded information about the background of the automaker's decision to try to grow rubber in Brazil, and about how things went from his point of view. Several articles published during the Fordlândia/Belterra period, in such journals as the *Bulletin* of the Pan-American Union, confirm the impression of Ford's infallibility that prevailed at the time. Wagley's works, chiefly his *Introduction to Brazil*, yield background on the nation's uneven political evolution from 1920 to the suicide of Getúlio Vargas in 1954. No one else should be blamed for shortcomings in my analysis of subsequent political and economic developments in Brazil; most of what is stated here about the period up to 1967 is culled from my files to *Time* written during the mid-1960s. Since then I have maintained a close interest in Brazil and have read widely, both in the popular press and in scholarly journals, about events there. The allegations and conclusions are my own. For deeper coverage of recent political trends in Brazil, I would particularly recommend the article in the Summer 1983 issue of *The Wilson Quarterly* by Riordan Roett, director of the Center of Brazilian Studies at the School of Advanced International Studies, Johns Hopkins University. In the late 1970s, Roett's institution and the one I then headed, the Center for Inter-American Relations, in New York, co-sponsored a private Commission on United States–Brazilian Relations. One prominent member of that commission was Albert Fishlow, an economist then at Yale University. Though not listed in the bibliography, his many papers and articles about the Brazilian economy have greatly added to my understanding of this complex subject.

With regard to the sections of the chapter that cover development schemes for the Amazon region during the period following the 1964 military coup, I gladly acknowledge assistance from many sources beyond my own knowledge and experience. Robert J. A. Goodland's many articles and the book of which he is a co-author, *Amazon Jungle: Green Hell to Red Desert*, contain authoritative coverage of the late 1960s and early 1970s. Emilio Moran's *Developing the Amazon* focuses tightly on the results of the early colonization efforts along the Trans-Amazon Highway. Papers presented at two scholarly conferences also proved highly useful. One, entitled "Land, People and Planning in Contemporary Amazonia," was held in 1979 at the University of Cambridge, England. Françoise Barbira-Scazzocchio was the editor of the conference proceedings subsequently issued. Another significant meeting, "Frontier Expansion in Amazonia," was held at the University of Florida, Gainesville, in February 1982. The papers presented, as edited by Marianne Schmink, provide comprehensive coverage of the subject. Though his conclusions differ from mine, I learned much from the journalist Jonathan Kandell's *Passage Through El Dorado*, a spirited account of the occupation of the South American continent's last frontiers. Norman Gall, a veteran American journalist who lives in São Paulo, wrote at length about Rondônia and other frontier regions in a series of papers published by the American Universities Field Service.

CHAPTER 6

I am fortunate to have had long and highly instructive conversations with many of the scientists whose work is reviewed in this chapter, and to have had an opportunity to read many of their books and articles. For further information about what they have published, please refer to the bibliography. Please note that, of all those mentioned, Sioli and Lovejoy have been the most willing to generalize about Amazonia beyond their particular fields of expertise.

CHAPTER 7

Once again, the bibliography includes references to the relevant published works of the scientists and researchers quoted or mentioned in this chapter. Particularly useful conversations or interviews took place with Philip Fearnside and Judy Rankin, João Murça Pires, Carl Jordan, and Susanna B. Hecht.

CHAPTER 8

A paper by Maria de Lourdes Davies de Freitas, chief environmentalist at the Companhia do Vale do Rio Doce, provides a succinct statement of the company's efforts to develop the iron-ore reserves at the Serra do Carajás in an ecologically sound manner. Official CVRD publications, as well as those of other companies including Eletronorte and Alumar, are the source of most of the facts and figures set forth about the so-called Grandes Projetos in Amazonia. Many articles in the popular press, particularly the *Wall Street Journal*, served as useful background for the material presented here. So did long conversations with many scientists—I should particularly mention Warwick Kerr, David Oren, Michael Goulding, and William Overal—about the effect of the grandly scaled development schemes on life in the basin. An alternative view is provided by Robert J. A. Goodland in his article entitled "Environmental Ranking of Amazonian Development Projects in Brazil."

CHAPTER 9

Fearnside and Herbert O. R. Schubart of INPA have closely studied the rates of deforestation in the Brazilian Amazon; their various articles are cited in the bibliography. Salati's continuing work on climate change is of prime importance; Meggers and Gentry have speculated about possible links between deforestation and flooding in Amazonia. Robert F. Skillings of the World Bank, a wise man who ran its Brazil desk for a decade, spent hours reviewing with me his thoughts about Amazonia's development potential—a subject he also covers in depth in an extensive analysis that he co-authored with Nils Tcheyan, then a graduate student at Johns Hopkins University's School of Advanced International Studies, now also a staff member at the World Bank. It would be manifestly unfair, however, to link these or any other sources with the judgments and conclusions offered here. They are fully mine, and I hope I am wrong.

BIBLIOGRAPHY

Acuña, Father Cristóbal de. *A New Discovery of the Great River of the Amazons, 1639*. First published in the Royal Press, Madrid, 1641. In *Expeditions into the Valley of the Amazons*. Edited by Clements R. Markham. New York: Burt Franklin Publishers (no date).

Agassiz, Louis. "Scientific Results of a Journey in Brazil." In *Geology and Physical Geography of Brazil*. Edited by Fred Hartt. Huntington, New York: Robert E. Krieger Publishing Company, 1975.

Agassiz, Louis, Mr. and Mrs. *A Journey in Brazil*. Cambridge (Mass.): University Press: Welch, Bigelow & Co., 1867.

Alvim, Paulo de T. "Agricultural Production Potential of the Amazon Region." In *Land, People and Planning in Contemporary Amazonia*. Proceedings of conference held September 23–26, 1979, Centre of Latin American Studies, Cambridge University. Cambridge: Cambridge Press, 1980.

"The Amazon: Saving the Last Frontier." *Time* cover story, October 18, 1982.

Barbira-Scazzocchio, Françoise. "From Native Forest to Private Property: The Development of Amazonia for Whom?" In *Land, People and Planning in Contemporary Amazonia*. Proceedings of conference held September 23–26, 1979, Centre of Latin American Studies, Cambridge University. Cambridge: Cambridge Press, 1980.

Barbira-Scazzocchio, Françoise, ed. *Land, People and Planning in Contemporary Amazonia*. Proceedings of conference held September 23–26, 1979, Centre of Latin American Studies, Cambridge University. Cambridge: Cambridge Press, 1980.

Bates, Henry Walter. *The Naturalist on the River Amazons*. Reprinted from the second edition. London: John Murray, 1864. Berkeley and Los Angeles: University of California Press (no date).

Bates, Marston. *The Forest and the Sea*. New York: Vintage Books, 1960.

Blowing in the Wind: Deforestation and Long Range Implications. Studies in Third World Societies Series 14. Williamsburg: Department of Anthropology, College of William and Mary, 1981.

Bourne, Richard. *Assault on the Amazon*. London: Victor Gollancz Ltd., 1978.

Boxer, C. R. *Four Centuries of Portuguese Expansion 1415–1825: A Succinct Survey*. Berkeley and Los Angeles: University of California Press, 1969.

Bryce, James Viscount. *South American Observations and Impressions*. London: Macmillan, 1912.

Bunker, Stephen G. "The Impact of Deforestation on Peasant Communities in the Medio Amazonas of Brazil." In *Where Have All the Flowers Gone? Deforestation in the Third World*. Studies in Third World Societies Series 13. Williamsburg: Department of Anthropology, College of William and Mary, 1981.

Camargo, Felisberto C. de. "Agricultura na América do Sul." In *Biogeography and Ecology in South America*. Edited by E. J. Fittkau, H. Klinge, and H. Sioli. The Hague: Dr. W. Junk, N.V. Publishers, 1968.

Cardoso, Fernando Henrique, and Geraldo Muller. *Amazônia: Expansão do Capitalismo*. São Paulo: Editora Brasiliense, S.A., 1978.

Carneiro, Edison. *A Conquista da Amazônia*. Rio de Janeiro: Ministerio da Viação e Obras Públicas, 1956.

Carneiro, Robert L. "Subsistence and Social Structure: An Ecological Study of the Kuimuru Indians." Doctoral dissertation, University of Michigan, 1957. Ann Arbor: University Microfilms International, 1979.

Carvajal, Friar Gaspar de. *The Discovery of the Amazon*. Introduction by Jose Toribio Medina. Edited by H. C. Heaton. New York: American Geographical Society, 1934.

Carvalho, José Cândido de Melo. *Considerações Sobre o Uso da Terra na Amazônia Brasileira*. Rio de Janeiro: Fundação Brasileira para a Conservação da Natureza, 1979.

Cochrane, Thomas T., and Pedro A. Sanchez. "Land Resources and Their Management in the Amazon Region: A State of Knowledge Report." In *Amazonia — Agriculture and Land Use Research*. Proceedings of CIAT Conference in Cali, Colombia. Edited by Susanna B. Hecht. Cali, Colombia: Centro Internacional de Agricultura Tropical, 1982.

"The Conservative Utilization of Tropical Forests." *Bulletin of the Pan-American Union*, September 1925.

Cook, J. Gordon. *Rubber*. London: Frederick Muller, Ltd., 1963.

Cunha, Euclides da. *À Margem da História* (second edition). Porto, Portugal: Livraria Chardron, 1913.

Davis, Shelton. *Victims of the Miracle*. New York: Cambridge University Press, 1977.

Denevan, William M. "Swiddens and Cattle Versus Forests: The Imminent Demise of the Amazon Rain Forest Reexamined." In *Where Have All the Flowers Gone? Deforestation in the Third World*. Studies in Third World Societies Series 13. Williamsburg: Department of Anthropology, College of William and Mary, 1981.

Dickinson, Robert E. "Effects of Tropical Deforestation on Climate." In *Blowing in the Wind: Deforestation and Long Range Implications*. Studies in Third World Societies Series 14. Williamsburg: Department of Anthropology, College of William and Mary, 1981.

Economist, The. "Ludwig's Dream of Amazon Riches Turns to Pulp." *The Economist*, December 26, 1981.

Edmundson, Rev. George M. A. *Brazil and Portugal*. Cambridge: Cambridge Modern History, 1907.

———. *The Voyage of Pedro Teixeira on the Amazon from Pará to Quito and Back*. London: Royal Historical Society Series 4, vol. 3, 1920.

Eidt, Robert C. "The Climatology of South America." In *Biogeography and Ecology in South America*. Edited by E. J. Fittkau, H. Klinge, and H. Sioli. The Hague: Dr. W. Junk, N.V. Publishers, 1968.

Empresa Brasileira de Pesquisa Agropecuária (EMBRAPA). *Conseqüências da Exploração Agropecuária Sobre as Condições Físicas e Químicas dos Solos das Microrregiões do Nordeste Paraense*. Belém, Pará: Centro de Pesquisa Agropecuária do Trópico Úmido, 1980.

Falesi, Ítalo Cláudio. *Ecossistema da Pastagem Cultivada na Amazônia Brasileira*. Belém, Pará: EMBRAPA, 1976.

———. "Soils of the Brazilian Amazon." In *Man in the Amazon*. Edited by Charles Wagley. Gainesville: University of Florida Press, 1974.

Fearnside, Philip M. "Cattle Yield Prediction for the Transamazon Highway of Brazil." *Interciencia*, July–August 1979. Caracas: Pergamon Press.

———. "The Effects of Cattle Pasture on Soil Fertility in the Brazilian Amazon: Consequences for Beef Production Sustainability." *Tropical Ecology* 21, 1 (1980).

———. "Stochastic Modeling in Human Carrying Capacity Estimation: A Tool for Development Planning in Amazonia." In *The Dilemma of Amazonian Development*. Edited by Emilio F. Moran. Boulder, Colorado: Westview Press, Inc., 1983.

———. "Transamazonian Highway, Brazil." In *Land, People and Planning in Contemporary Amazonia*. Proceedings of conference held September 23–26, 1979, Centre of Latin American Studies, Cambridge University. Cambridge: Cambridge Press, 1980.

Fearnside, Philip M., and Judy M. Rankin. "Jari and Carajás: The Uncertain Future of large Silvicultural Plantations in the Amazon." *Interciencia*, November-December 1982. Caracas: Pergamon Press.

———. "Jari and Development in the Brazilian Amazon." *Interciencia*, May–June 1980. Caracas: Pergamon Press.

———. "The New Jari: Risks and Prospects of a Major Amazonian Development." *Interciencia*, November–December 1982. Caracas: Pergamon Press.

Fittkau, E. J., and V. Irmler, W. J. Junk, F. Reiss, and G. W. Schmidt. "Productivity, Biomass and Population Dynamics in Amazonian Water Bodies." In *Tropical Ecological Systems*. Edited by Frank B. Golley and Ernesto Medina. New York: Springer-Verlag, 1975.

Fittkau, E. J., H. Klinge, and H. Sioli. *Biogeography and Ecology in South America*. The Hague: Dr. W. Junk, N.V. Publishers, 1968.

Fleming, Peter. *Brazilian Adventure*. London: Jonathan Cape, 1933.

Freitas, Maria de Lourdes Davies de, and Christine M. Smyrski-Schluger. *Brazil's Carajás Iron Ore Project: Environmental Aspects*. Rio de Janeiro: Companhia Vale do Rio Doce (CVRD), 1982.

Freyre, Gilberto. *Order and Progress: Brazil from Monarchy to Republic*. Edited and translated by Rod W. Horton. New York: Alfred A. Knopf, 1970.

Furneaux, Robin. *The Amazon, the Story of a Great River*. London: Hamish Hamilton, 1969.

Gall, Norman. "Brazil on the Brink." *Forbes Magazine*, February 4, 1980.

———. *Letter from Rondônia: A Five-Part Series*. Hanover, New Hampshire: American Universities Field Staff, 1978.

———. "Ludwig's Amazon Empire." *Forbes Magazine*, May 14, 1979.

Gentry, Alwyn H. "Deforestation and Increased Flooding of the Upper Amazon." *Science*, December 19, 1980, and January 22, 1982.

Goeldi, Emílio A. *Alexandre Rodrigues Ferreira*. Brasília: Editora Universidade de Brasília, 1982.

Golley, Frank B., and Ernesto Medina, eds. *Tropical Ecological Systems*. Ecological Studies, vol. 2. New York: Springer-Verlag, 1975.

Goodland, Robert J. A. "Brazil's Environmental Progress in Amazonian Development." Draft paper presented at 44th International Congress of Americanists, Manchester, England, September 6, 1982.

———. *Environmental Ranking of Amazonian Development Projects in Brazil*. Switzerland: Environmental Conservation, the Foundation for Environmental Conservation, Spring 1980.

Goodland, Robert J. A., and Howard S. Irwin. *Amazon Jungle: Green Hell to Red Desert?* New York: Elsevier Scientific Publishing Company, 1975.

———. "Amazonian Forest and Cerrado: Development and Environmental Considerations." In *Extinction Is Forever*. Edited by Ghillean T. Prance and Thomas S. Elias. New York: The New York Botanical Garden, 1977.

Goodman, Edward J. *The Explorers of South America*. New York: The Macmillan Company, 1972.

Goulding, Michael. *The Fishes and the Forest: Explorations in Amazonian Natural History*. Berkeley, Los Angeles, and London: University of California Press, 1980.

Gross, Daniel, ed. *Peoples and Cultures of Native South America*. Published for the American Museum of Natural History. Garden City: Doubleday/The Natural History Press, 1973.

Haffer, Jurgen. "General Aspects of the Refuge Theory." In *Biological Model of Diversification in the Tropics*. Edited by Ghillean T. Prance. New York: Columbia University Press, 1983.

————. "Speciation in Amazonian Forest Birds." *Science*, July 11, 1969.

Hanson, Earl Parker. *Journey to Manaus*. New York: Reynal and Hitchcock, 1938.

Hanson, Earl Parker, ed. *South from the Spanish Main: South America Seen Through the Eyes of Its Discoverers*. New York: Delacorte Press, 1967.

Hartshorn, Gary S. "Take the Profits and Run." *Garden*, January–February 1982.

Haskins, Caryl P. *The Amazon: A Life History of a Mighty River*. Garden City: Doubleday, Doran & Company, Inc., 1943.

Hecht, Susanna B. "Deforestation in the Amazon Basin: Magnitude, Dynamics and Soil Resource Effects." In *Where Have All the Flowers Gone? Deforestation in the Third World*. Studies in Third World Societies Series 13. Williamsburg: Department of Anthropology, College of William and Mary, 1981.

Hecht, Susanna B., ed. *Amazonia: Agriculture and Land Use Research*. Proceedings of CIAT Conference, 1980. Cali, Colombia: Centro Internacional de Agricultura Tropical, 1982.

Hemming, John. *Red Gold: The Conquest of the Brazilian Indians 1500–1760*. Cambridge (Mass.): Harvard University Press, 1978.

"Henry Ford as a Rubber Grower." *The Outlook* 147, no. 8 (October 26, 1927).

Herrera, Rafael, Carl F. Jordan, Ernesto Medina, and Hans Klinge. "How Human Activities Disturb the Nutrient Cycles of a Tropical Rainforest in Amazonia." *AMBIO* (Journal of Human Environment). Uppsala: Swedish Academy of Sciences, 1981.

Hester, James J. "Late Pleistocene Environments and Early Man in South America." In *Peoples and Cultures in Native South America*. Edited by Daniel R. Gross. Published for the American Museum of Natural History. Garden City: Doubleday/The Natural History Press, 1973.

Hoge, Warren. "A General Loosens the Reins in Brazil." *The New York Times Magazine*, December 6, 1981.

Humboldt, Baron Alexander von, and Aimé Bonpland. *Personal Narrative of Travels to the Equinoctial Regions of the New Continent During the Years 1799–1804*. 6 vols. London: Longman, Hurst, Rees, 1808. Reprinted New York: AMA Press, Inc., 1966.

Ianni, Octávio. *Colonização e Contra-Reforma Agrária na Amazônia*. Petrópolis: Editora Vozes Ltda., 1979.

Institute for Cross-Cultural Research. *Indians of Brazil in the Twentieth Century, ICR Studies 2*. Washington: Institute for Cross-Cultural Research, 1967.

Instituto Brasileiro de Análises Sociais e Econômicas. *Carajás: O Brasil Hipoteca Seu Futuro*. Rio de Janeiro: Edições Achiame Ltda., 1983.

Instituto National de Pesquisas da Amazônia (INPA). *Estratégias Para Politica Florestal na Amazônia Brasileira*. Manaus: *Acta Amazônica*, December 1979.

"International Cooperation by Scientific Agencies in Tropical Forestry." *Bulletin of the Pan-American Union*, July 1925.

Jenny, Hans. "Causes of the High Nitrogen and Organic Matter Content of Certain Tropical Forest Soils." *Soil Science* 69 (1950). New Brunswick: Rutgers University.

———. "Great Soil Groups in the Equatorial Regions of Colombia, South America." *Soil Science* 66 (1948). New Brunswick: Rutgers University.

Jordan, Carl F. "Amazon Rain Forests." *American Scientist*, July–August 1982.

———. *The Environmental Consequences of Intensive Forestry and the Removal of Whole Trees from Forests*. Proceedings of the MAB Conference on Biological and Sociological Basis for Rational Use of Forest Resources for Energy and Organics, Michigan State University, East Lansing, May 6–11, 1979.

Jordan, Carl F., and Rafael Herrera. "Tropical Rain Forests: Are Nutrients Really Critical?" *The American Naturalist*, February 1981.

Kandell, Jonathan. *Passage Through El Dorado*. New York: William Morrow and Company, Inc., 1984.

Key, Pierre V. R. *Enrico Caruso, a Biography*. Boston: Little Brown, 1922.

Kinkead, Gwen. "Trouble in D. K. Ludwig's Jungle." *Fortune*, April 20, 1981.

Klein, Odacir, Luís Carlos Lopes Madeira, Marcos Dantas, and Marcelo Cordeiro. *Salvar Carajás*. Porto Alegre, Brazil: L+PM Editores Ltda., 1982.

Klinge, Hans, W. A. Rodrigues, E. Brunig, and E. J. Fittkau. "Biomass and Structure in a Central Amazonian Rain Forest." In *Tropical Ecological Systems*. Edited by Frank B. Golley and Ernesto Medina. New York: Springer-Verlag, 1975.

Leão, Velloso. *Euclides da Cunha na Amazônia*. Rio de Janeiro: Livraria São José, 1966.

Lovejoy, Thomas E. "Hope for a Beleaguered Paradise." *Garden*, January–February 1982.

Lovejoy, Thomas E., R. O. Bierregaard, J. M. Rankin, and H. O. R. Schubart. "Ecological Dynamics of Forest Fragments." In *Tropical Rain Forest: Ecology and Management*. Edited by S. L. Sutton, T. C. Whitmore, and A. C. Chadwick. Oxford: Blackwell Scientific Publications, 1983.

Lovejoy, Thomas E., and David C. Oren. "Minimum Critical Size of Ecosystems." Paper presented at the annual meeting of the American Institute of Biological Sciences, Michigan State University, East Lansing, August 25, 1977.

Lovejoy, Thomas E., and Eneas Salati. "Precipitating Change in Amazonia." In *The Dilemma of Amazonian Development*. Edited by Emilio F. Moran. Boulder, Colorado: Westview Press, Inc., 1983.

Lovejoy, Thomas E., and H. O. R. Schubart. "The Ecology of Amazonian Development." In *Land, People and Planning in Contemporary Amazonia*. Proceedings of conference held September 23–26, 1979. Edited by F. Barbira-Scazzocchio.

Centre of Latin American Studies, Cambridge University. Cambridge: Cambridge Press, 1980.

Mahar, Dennis J. *Frontier Development Policy in Brazil: A Study of Amazonia*. New York: Praeger Publishers, 1979.

———. "Public International Lending Institutions and the Development of the Brazilian Amazon: The Experience of the World Bank." Prepared for the Conference of Frontier Expansion in Amazonia, Center for Latin American Studies, University of Florida, Gainesville, February 8–11, 1982.

Markham, Clements R. *Expeditions into the Valley of the Amazons*, 1539, 1540, 1639. Originally published by the Hakluyt Society. New York: Burt Franklin Publishers.

Meggers, Betty J. *Amazonia: Man and Culture in a Counterfeit Paradise*. Chicago: Aldine-Atherton, Inc., 1971.

———. "Environment and Culture in Amazonia." In *Man in the Amazon*. Edited by Charles Wagley. Gainesville: University of Florida Press, 1974.

———. "Explaining the Course of Human Events." In *How Humans Adapt: A Biocultural Odyssey*. Edited by Donald J. Ortner. Washington: Smithsonian Press, 1983.

———. "Vegetational Fluctuation and Prehistoric Cultural Adaptation in Amazonia: Some Tentative Correlations." *World Archaeology* 8, no. 3 (February 1977).

Meggers, Betty J., Edward Ayensu, and W. Donald Duckworth, eds. *Tropical Forest Ecosystems in Africa and South America: A Comparative Review*. Washington: Smithsonian Press, 1973.

Metraux, Alfred. "Tribes of the Middle and Upper Amazon River." *Handbook of the South American Indians* 3. Edited by Julian H. Steward. Washington: The Smithsonian Institution, 1948.

Meyer-Abich, Adolf. "Humboldt's Exploration in the American Tropics." *The Texas Quarterly* (no date).

Moran, Emilio F. "The Adaptive System of the Amazonian Caboclo." In *Man in the Amazon*. Edited by Charles Wagley. Gainesville: University of Florida Press, 1974.

———. "Colonization in the Transamazon and Rondonia." Presented at the Conference on Frontier Expansion in Amazonia, Center for Latin American Studies, University of Florida, Gainesville, February 8–11, 1982.

———. *Developing the Amazon*. Bloomington: Indiana University Press, 1981.

———. *The Dilemma of Amazonian Development*. Boulder, Colorado: Westview Press, Inc., 1983.

———. "Ecological, Anthropological and Agronomic Research in the Amazon Basin." *Latin American Research Review* 17, no. 1 (1982). Chapel Hill: University of North Carolina.

———. "Mobility and Resource Use in Amazonia." In *Land, People and Planning in Contemporary Amazonia*. Proceedings of conference held September 23–26, 1979, Centre of Latin American Studies, Cambridge University. Cambridge: Cambridge Press, 1980.

Morison, Samuel Eliot. *The European Discovery of America: The Southern Voyages 1492–1616*. New York: Oxford University Press, 1974.

Myers, Norman. "Deforestation in the Tropics: Who Gains, Who Loses?" In *Where Have All the Flowers Gone? Deforestation in the Third World*. Studies in Third World Societies Series 13. Williamsburg: Department of Anthropology, College of William and Mary, 1981.

———. *The Sinking Ark*. Oxford: Pergamon Press, 1979.

Nevins, Allan, and Frank Ernest Hill. *Ford: Expansion and Challenge —1915–1933*. New York: Charles Scribner's Sons, 1957.

Nogueira Neto, Paulo. *A Explosão Demográfica e O Meio Ambiente*. Rio de Janeiro: Fundação Brasileira para a Conservação da Natureza, 1979.

Oldfield, Margery L. "Tropical Deforestation and Genetic Resources Conservation." In *Blowing in the Wind: Deforestation and Long Range Implications*. Studies in Third World Societies Series 14. Williamsburg: Department of Anthropology, College of William and Mary, 1981.

Pandolfo, Clara. *Ecology and Development in Amazonia*. Belém, Pará: Superintendencia do Desenvolvimento da Amazônia (SUDAM), Departamento de Recursos Naturais, 1982.

"Para Rubber Making." *Scientific American*, July 18, 1891.

Pinto, Lúcio Flávio. *Amazônia: No Rastro do Saque*. São Paulo: Editora Hucitec, 1980.

Pires, João Murça, and Ghillean T. Prance. *The Amazon Forest: A Natural Heritage to Be Preserved*. In *Extinction Is Forever*. Edited by Ghillean T. Prance and Thomas S. Elias. New York: The New York Botanical Garden, 1977.

Pompermayer, M. J. "The State and Frontier in Brazil." Doctoral dissertation, Stanford University, 1979.

Posey, Darrell A. "The Keepers of the Forest." *Garden*, January–February 1982.

Prance, Ghillean T. "The Amazon: The Earth's Most Dazzling Forest." *Garden*, January–February 1982.

———, ed. *Biological Model of Diversification in the Tropics*. New York: Columbia University Press, 1983.

Prance, Ghillean T., and Thomas S. Elias, eds. *Extinction Is Forever: The Status of Threatened and Endangered Plants of the Americas*. New York: The New York Botanical Garden, 1977.

Rabelo, Genival. *Ocupação da Amazonia*. Rio de Janeiro: Empresa Jornalística P.N., S.A., 1968.

Rangel, Alberto. *Inferno Verde*. Rio de Janeiro: Tipográfia Minerva, 1914.

Rau, Charles. *Memoirs of C. F. P. von Martius*. Washington: U.S. Government Printing Office, 1871.

Reis, Arthur César Ferreira. *A Amazônia e a Cobiça Internacional*. Rio de Janeiro: Edinova Limitada, 1960.

———. *A Amazônia Que os Portugueses Revelaram*. Rio de Janeiro: Ministério da Educação e Cultura, 1956.

———. "Economic History of the Brazilian Amazon." In *Man in the Amazon*.

Edited by Charles Wagley. Gainesville: University of Florida Press, 1974.

———. *O Descobrimento da Amazônia*. Belém, Pará: DEIP, 1942.

Ribeiro, Darcy. *Os Índios e a Civilização*. Petrópolis: Editora Vozes Ltda., 1979.

Ribeiro, Maria de Nazaré Goes, Eneas Salati, Nilson Augusto Villa Nova, and Clarice G. B. Demétrio. *Radiação Solar Disponível em Manaus (AM) e Sua Relação Com a Duração do Brilho Solar. Acta Amazônica* 12(2). Manaus: Instituto Nacional de Pesquisas Amazônicas (INPA), 1982.

Richards, P. W. "Speciation in the Tropical Rain Forest and the Concept of the Niche." *Biological Journal of the Linnean Society* 1 (1969), London.

———. *The Tropical Rain Forest: An Ecological Study*. Cambridge: The University Press, 1952.

Rodrigues Ferreira, Alexandre. *Viagem Filosófica pelas Captanias do Grão Pará, Rio Negro, Mato Grosso e Cuiabá, 1783–1792*. Rio de Janeiro: Reissued by Conselho Federal de Cultura, 1971.

Roett, Riordan. "Staying the Course." *The Wilson Quarterly* (Summer 1983). Washington: The Smithsonian Institution.

Roosevelt, Anna Curtenius. *Parmana: Prehistoric Maize and Manioc Subsistence Along the Amazon and Orinoco*. New York: Academic Press, Inc., 1980.

Roosevelt, Theodore. *Through the Brazilian Wilderness*. New York: Charles Scribner's Sons, 1919.

"Rubber Cultivation in Brazil." *Bulletin of the Pan-American Union*, July 1918.

Sanchez, Pedro A. "Soils of the Humid Tropics." In *Blowing in the Wind: Deforestation and Long Range Implications*. Studies in Third World Societies Series 14. Williamsburg: Department of Anthropology, College of William and Mary, 1981.

Sanchez, Pedro A., Dale E. Bandy, J. Hugo Villachica, and John J. Nicholaides. "Amazon Basin Soils: Management for Continuous Crop Production." *Science* 216 (May 21, 1982).

Sanchez, Pedro A., and L. E. Tergas. *Pasture Production in Acid Soils of the Tropics*. Proceedings of a seminar held at CIAT, Cali, Colombia, April 17–21, 1978. Cali, Colombia: Centro Internacional de Agricultura Tropical, 1979.

Santos, Roberto Aráujo de Oliveira. *História Econômica da Amazônia, 1800–1920*. T. A. Queiróz, Editor, Ltda., São Paulo, 1980.

Saunders, John. "The Population of the Brazilian Amazon Today." In *Man in the Amazon*. Edited by Charles Wagley. Gainesville: University of Florida Press, 1974.

Schultes, R. A. *Plants of the Gods*. New York: McGraw-Hill, 1980.

Shane, Douglas R. *Hoofprints on the Forest: An Inquiry into the Beef Cattle Industry in the Tropical Forest Areas of Latin America*. Washington: Office of Environmental Affairs, U.S. Department of State, 1980.

Shreve, Forrest. "The Direct Effects of Rainfall on Hygraphilous Vegetation." *The Journal of Ecology*, vol. 2. London: British Ecological Society, 1914.

Sioli, Harald. "Foreseeable Consequences of Actual Development Schemes and Alternative Ideas." In *Land, People and Planning in Contemporary Amazonia*.

Proceedings of conference held September 23–26, 1979, Centre of Latin American Studies, Cambridge University. Edited by F. Barbira-Scazzocchio. Cambridge: Cambridge Press, 1980.

———. "Recent Activities in the Brazilian Amazon Region and Their Ecological Effects." In *Tropical Forest Ecosystems in Africa and South America: A Comparative Review.* Edited by Betty J. Meggers, Edward Ayensu, and W. Donald Duckworth. Washington: The Smithsonian Institution, 1973.

———. "Tropical Rivers as Expressions of Their Terrestrial Environments." In *Tropical Ecological Systems.* Edited by Frank B. Golley and Ernesto Medina. New York: Springer-Verlag, 1975.

Skillings, Robert F., and Nils Tcheyan. *Economic Development Prospects of the Amazon Region of Brazil.* Paper prepared at the School of Advanced International Studies, Johns Hopkins University, 1979.

Smith, Nigel J. H. "Colonization Lessons from a Tropical Forest." *Science*, November 13, 1981.

———. "Human Exploitation of Terra Firme/Fauna in Amazonia." *Ciencia e Cultura*, January 30, 1978.

Souza, Márcio. *A Expressão Amazonense.* São Paulo: Editora Alfa-Omega, 1978.

Spix, Johann Baptist von, and Karl Friedrich von Martius. *Travels in Brazil in the Years 1817–1820.* London: Longman, Hurst, Rees, 1824.

Spruce, Richard. *Notes of a Botanist on the Amazon.* Edited by A. R. Wallace. London: Macmillan and Company, 1908.

Sweet, David Graham. "A Rich Realm of Nature Destroyed: The Middle Amazon Valley, 1640–1750." Doctoral dissertation, the University of Wisconsin, 1974. Ann Arbor: University Microfilms, 1983.

Tocantins, Leandro. *Amazônia—Natureza, Homen e Tempo.* Second edition, revised and enlarged. Rio de Janeiro: Editora Civilização Brasileira, 1982.

———. "The World of the Amazon Region." In *Man in the Amazon.* Edited by Charles Wagley. Gainesville: University of Florida Press, 1974.

"The Tropical Forestry Problem." *Bulletin of the Pan-American Union*, August 1925.

Uhl, Christopher. *Recovery Following Disturbances of Different Intensities in the Amazon Rain Forest of Venezuela.* Caracas: International Amazon Project, Ecology Center, Instituto Venezolano de Investigaciones Científicas (no date).

———. "You Can't Keep a Good Forest Down." *Natural History*, April 1983.

Valverde, Orlando, and Tácito Lívio Reis de Freitas. *O Problema Florestal na Amazônia Brasileira.* Petrópolis: Editora Vozes Ltda., 1980.

Vanzolini, P. E. "Paleoclimates, Relief and Species Multiplication in Equatorial Forests." In *Tropical Forest Ecosystems in Africa and South America: A Comparative Review.* Edited by Betty J. Meggers, et al. Washington: The Smithsonian Institution, 1973.

Veríssimo, José. *Estudos Amazônicos.* Belém, Pará: Universidade Federal do Pará, 1970.

Vickers, William Taylor. "Cultural Adaptation to Amazonian Habitats: The Siona-

Secoya of Eastern Ecuador." Doctoral dissertation, the University of Florida, 1976. Ann Arbor: University Microfilms, 1977.

Von Hagen, Victor Wolfgang. *The Green World of the Naturalists*. New York: Greenberg, 1948.

————. *South America Called Them: Explorations of the Great Naturalists*. New York: Alfred A. Knopf, 1945.

Wagley, Charles. *Amazon Town*. New York: Alfred A. Knopf, 1953 (revised 1964).

————. *An Introduction to Brazil*. New York: Columbia University Press, 1963.

Wagley, Charles, ed. *Man in the Amazon*. Gainesville: The University of Florida Press, 1974.

Wallace, Alfred Russel. *A Narrative of Travels on the Amazon and Rio Negro*. London: Ward, Lock & Co., 1889.

Where Have All the Flowers Gone? Deforestation in the Third World. Studies in Third World Societies Series 13. Williamsburg: Department of Anthropology, College of William and Mary, 1981.

Woodwell, George M. "The Challenge of Endangered Species." In *Extinction Is Forever*. Edited by Ghillean T. Prance and Thomas S. Elias. New York: The New York Botanical Garden, 1977.

Woodwell, G. M., J. E. Hobbie, R. A. Houghton, J. M. Melillo, B. Moore, B. J. Petersen, and G. R. Shaver. "Global Deforestation: Contribution to Atmospheric Carbon Dioxide." *Science*, December 9, 1983.

World Bank. *The Integrated Development of Brazil's Northwest Frontier*. Washington, December 23, 1980.

Wright, Marie Robinson. *The New Brazil: Its Resources and Attractions; Historical, Descriptive and Industrial*. Philadelphia: George Barrie and Son, 1901.

INDEX

Roots, 67, 108, 114–15
Rotation systems, 122–23
Rubber, 24, 53, 54, 58, 67, 95, 105, 106, 153, 156, 158; era, 70, 73, 75–76, 78–82

Salati, Eneas, 115–16, 138, 150, 152, 153
Salesian missionaries, 3, 14
San Carlos, 11, 21, 114
Sanchez, Pedro A., 122–23, 125
Santarém, 11, 25, 63, 78, 79
São Gabriel, 3–15, 21–23
São Joaquim, 3, 13–14
São Luís, 2, 45, 48, 94, 131–37, 141
São Paulo, 38, 93, 119, 155
São Raimundo, 124
Sapopemas, 67
Schimper, A. F. W., 67
Schistosomiasis, 138
Schubart, Herbert, 150, 152, 157–158, 161
Schultes, Richard E., 128
Seed dispersal, 66, 112
Seringueiros, 76
Serra Norte, 142, 144, 145
Serra Pelada, 144
Silviculture, 124, 127, 158, 159
Sioli, Harald, 75, 107–8, 115, 116, 119, 127, 153
Skillings, Robert F., 90, 156
Slash and burn, 31, 120, 121, 160
Slavery, 33, 44, 48, 49, 51, 57, 68, 69, 131
Smith, Nigel, 129
Smithsonian Institution, 24, 101, 112
Soil(s), 5, 20, 49, 88; contemporary studies and conservation efforts, 101, 103, 106–8, 115, 120–30, 139, 149–63; nineteenth-century studies, 61, 65, 67; nutrient-loss problem, 121–24; prehistoric, 27
Solimões, 1, 2, 22, 29, 31, 33, 60,

61, 63, 65, 88, 107, 108
South America: discovery of, 35; formation of continent, 25–26
Soybeans, 93, 123
Spanish exploration and colonization, 33, 35–48, 54, 56
Species, 28, 99, 108–9; contemporary studies and conservation efforts, 98–116, 120–30, 139, 149–63; effects of development on, 75–76, 88, 90, 99, 118–48, 149–63; endangered, 47, 112, 129, 153–54, 162–63; nineteenth-century studies, 60–67; undiscovered, 153–54. See also specific species
Spix, Johann Baptist von, 60, 61
Spruce, Richard, 3–4, 9, 12, 13, 15–16, 63, 65–67, 106
Squatters, 95, 136–37, 159
Steel, 82, 91, 134
Subsistence farming, 123, 136
SUDAM, 85, 90, 91, 147, 157, 161
SUFRAMA, 98
Sugar, 47, 49, 75
Sweet, David Graham, 31, 49

Tabatinga, 29, 60
Tapajós, 11, 78, 79, 88, 108, 159
Taraqua, 17
Tcheyan, Nils, 95–96
Teixeira, Pedro de, 45, 46, 51
Terra firme, 27, 106–7, 123, 130
Tertiary period, 108, 111
Thayer expedition, 69–70
Tin, 93, 146
Tocantins River, 88, 94, 107, 137, 138, 139
Toledo, Andrés de, 45
Tomé-Açu, 119
Tordesillas, Treaty of, 38, 43, 46, 51
Toucanos, 16
Trans-Amazon Highway, 88, 90, 153
Trombetas River, 93, 94, 146, 147
Trovão, 14, 15, 16

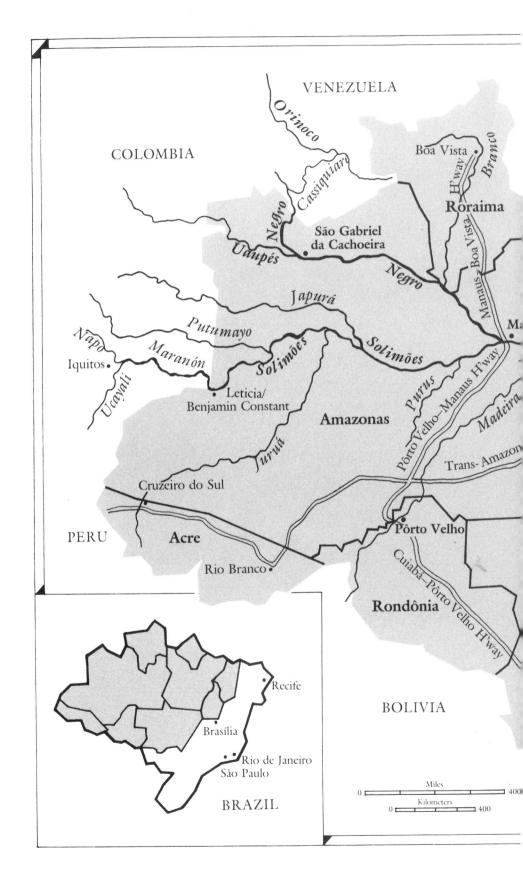